CW00524079

# DAHLIAS

First published in the United Kingdom in 2018 by
Pavilion
43 Great Ormond Street
London
WC1N 3HZ



ISBN 978-1-911595-25-0

A CIP catalogue record for this book is available from the British Library.

10 9 8 7 6 5 4 3 2

Reproduction by Mission Productions, Hong Kong
Printed and bound by 1010 Printing International Ltd, China

www.pavilionbooks.com

# DAHLIAS

**NAOMI SLADE**
photography by
**GEORGIANNA LANE**

PAVILION

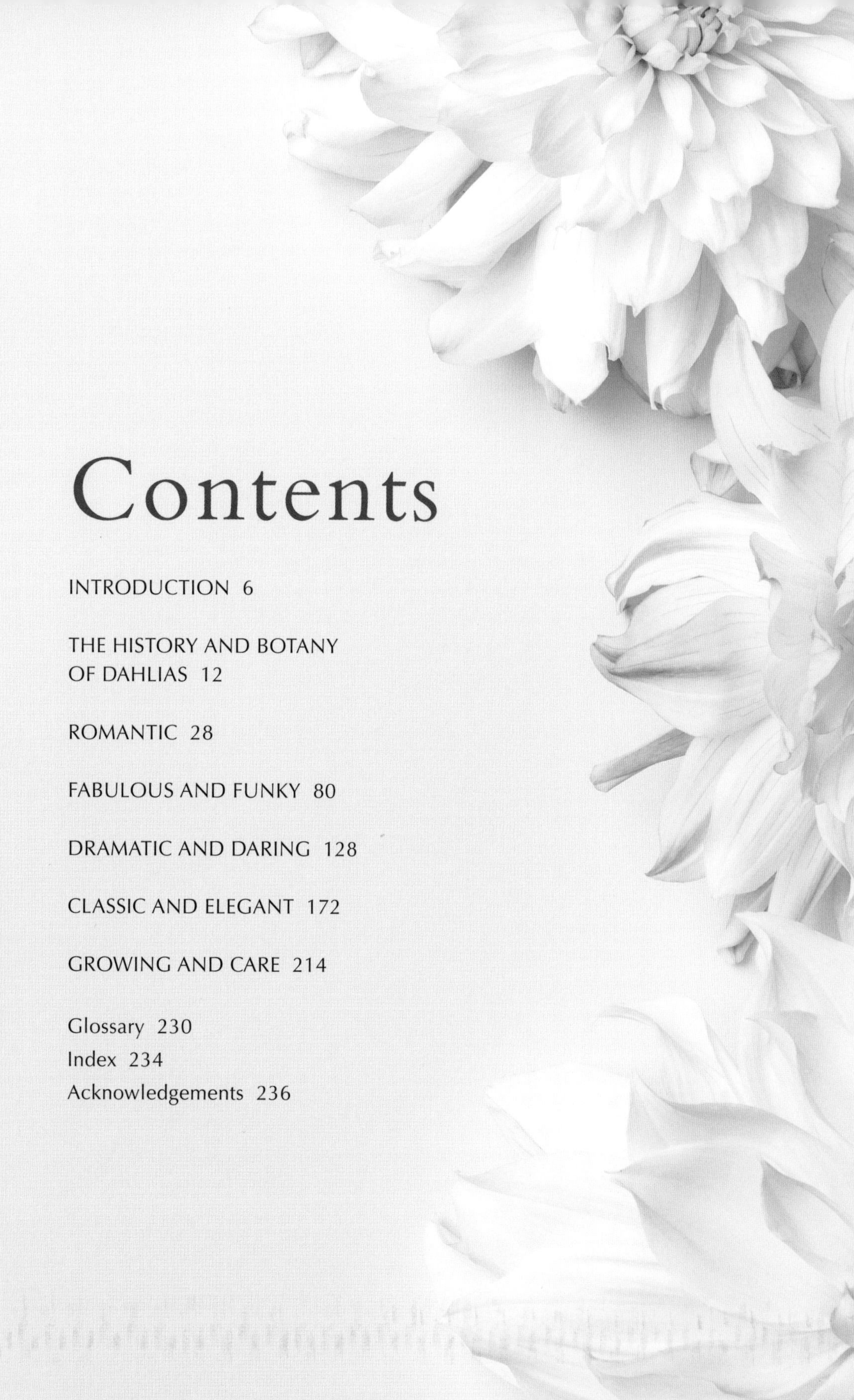

# Contents

# INTRODUCTION

THERE IS NOTHING AVERAGE ABOUT DAHLIAS. THEY ARE FLOWERS WITH PIZZAZZ AND PURPOSE, OOZING PERSONALITY AND CHARACTER. THE BOLD, CHEERFUL COLOURS ENGAGE YOU DESPITE YOURSELF; THE FEISTY, DRAMATIC SHAPES SEEK TO STARTLE AND THE INTENSE, MATHEMATICAL FLOWER FORMS CAPTIVATE. LOVE THEM OR HATE THEM, IT IS JUST NOT POSSIBLE TO LOOK A WELL-GROWN DAHLIA IN THE EYE AND FEEL NOTHING FOR IT.

Dahlias inspire wanderlust. For all their flamboyance in the garden and for all the lush softness that makes them so suitable for bridal bouquets and babies, for me, they represent a road less travelled.

I want to climb mountains in Mexico and discover wild dahlias in their most remote refuges. Rejoice as they flourish untamed in their own bright and humid summer. Watch as they crumble and collapse, familiar yet strange, in the light, sharp frost of their upland winter.

To see a plant in its natural environment makes my skin tingle with excitement. Particularly a plant such as this, borne into cultivation through conquest, empire and exploitation, yet with aeons of inherent significance and ethno-botanical custom before it. A whole history of evolution and use that may never make the daily news, but is nonetheless fascinating.

As the Spanish penetrated Central America, their explorers chanced upon many wonderful things. Among them was a strange and vivacious plant, with fine flowers and promiscuous tendencies. Pounced upon by hybridizers, new forms and colours proliferated at prodigious speed and dahlias became the darlings of the European masses. Adoration of their overblown fabulousness peaked with the Victorians, as bedding plants and the stars of horticultural shows, but, as the twentieth century wore on, they fell from favour. The vivid colours and large sizes became vulgar, and achieving show-bench perfection became unappealingly intensive.

But the world turns and fashions change. In the last 20 years, dahlias have seen a revival, with the diverse and joyful flowers once more welcomed to borders and bouquets. The newly developed Single forms are charming and sophisticated, the great frilly Dinner-Plates, lush and lavish.

And this takes us back to Mexico. Of the 36 or so species of dahlia, garden cultivars have largely arisen as hybrids of the few that first arrived in Europe – variable plants that mutated freely, yielding a palimpsest of colour and form. And a large part of our renewed interest has arisen because modern explorers, plant hunters and intellectual conquistadors returned to the mountains. Emerging filled with fire and dreams, they crossed plants that are horticulturally rare but filled with genetic potential, with established garden staples.

The results are closer to the wild type, with richly coloured, finely cut leaves and single flowers, an atavistic delicacy of form that has provided gardeners with something freshly relevant.

Dahlias have many charms and foibles. They are, for example, unscented. The tubers are edible and are sometimes marketed as 'dahlia yams' although, as a foodstuff, the texture is odd, the flavour average, and the storage carbohydrate – inulin – can cause unfortunate bloating in the uninitiated.

They remain locally significant as the national flower of Mexico, yet single dahlias appeared in Aztec rituals, depicting both the flower and the sun with rays around a blazing core. They also had medical significance, yielding 'Atlantic starch' – an early sugar substitute for diabetics. In the 'language of flowers', they meant compassion, respect, dignity and elegance, and in some quarters, a bond that will last forever – doubtless fuelling our contemporary enthusiasm for dahlia wedding bouquets.

Yet, despite the magnificent, flaming blooms and the miraculous, almost impossible vigour that dahlias can achieve at their best, they link clearly to the cycles of life. That delicate, fleshy, late-spring emergence, the robust, powerful, growth spurt, a blaze of glory all summer long, and then the poignant sense of a life and a season at its end. 'Frost To-night', by the American poet Edith M. Thomas (1854–1925) puts it well:

> Apple-green west and an orange bar,
> And the crystal eye of a lone, one star …
> And, 'Child, take the shears and cut what
> you will,
> Frost to-night – so clear and dead-still.'
>
> Then I sally forth, half sad, half proud,
> And I come to the velvet, imperial crowd,
> The wine-red, the gold, the crimson, the
> pied, –
> The dahlias that reign by the garden-side.
> The dahlias I might not touch till to-night!
> A gleam of the shears in the fading light,
> And I gathered them all, – the splendid
> throng,
> And in one great sheaf I bore them along.
>
> In my garden of Life with its all late flowers
> I heed a Voice in the shrinking hours:
> 'Frost to-night – so clear and dead-still' …
> Half sad, half proud, my arms I fill.

In this book I share my passion for these beautiful, astonishing, versatile flowers and hope to inspire a hunger in others to spread their wings and experiment. There is a flower for every taste, no matter how conservative or outlandish that taste may be, and there is no colour scheme for which a dahlia cannot be found to suit. And if you fall in love, then growing dahlias is a pastime that will last you until the end of days.

Tens of thousands of cultivars exist, and it has been proven time and again that a fresh eye can reveal new delights. New breeding brings new introductions every year – compact, versatile, innovative plants that throw dahlias once more into the spotlight. From the smallest patch of garden, filled with ambition and hope, this is a plant to intrigue and inspire. And as I climb the verdant mountains of my imagination, my heart sings.

# THE HISTORY AND BOTANY OF DAHLIAS

CONQUERORS OF FAR-FLUNG PLACES USUALLY TAKE WITH THEM A FAIRLY PREDICTABLE SHOPPING LIST. LAND, GOLD AND EMPIRE ARE ALL HIGHLY ACCEPTABLE PRIZES. THERE CAN BE ALL MANNER OF ESOTERIC ADD-ONS, SUCH AS NEW FOODS OR EXOTIC SPICES, WHICH MIGHT CONFER AN ECONOMIC ADVANTAGE. BUT VERY OFTEN, THE PLUCKY EXPLORERS MAKE OTHER DISCOVERIES, TOO.

When the conquistadors arrived in Mexico and Central America in 1525, they found the indigenous people collecting and cultivating an intriguing local flower. Known as *acocotli* or *cocoxochitl* in the languages of the region, it had hollow stems that were perfect for piping water, and the name could be loosely translated as 'the water-pipe plant'.

The plant was also used therapeutically to treat epilepsy and the plump tuber was exploited as a food crop by the Aztecs. It is likely that the hopeful explorers may have sent it to Spain as a potential rival to that other notable tuber, the potato. But while the new plant looked better in bloom, it lacked merit in the kitchen and was quietly forgotten until 1570, when physician Francisco Hernández de Toledo was ordered to Mexico by King Philip II to study its plants.

Reporting back, Hernández described two dahlia types, a single flower similar to *Dahlia pinnata* and the enormous *Dahlia imperialis*. His account, illustrated by Francisco Domínguez, also shows other dahlias. These bear a resemblance to the species *Dahlia merckii* and the modern bedding dahlia, and, from the drawing, some of them are clearly partially double.

Yet, surprisingly, dahlias did not reach Europe until 1789, when Vicente Cervantes, Director of the Botanical Garden in Mexico City, sent plant material to Antonio José Cavanilles, Director of the Royal Gardens in Madrid. The new genus was named to honour the Swedish botanist Anders Dahl, who had died that year, and as the plants flowered, Cavanilles identified three species. These he named *Dahlia pinnata*, after its pinnate foliage, *D. rosea* for its pinky-purple bloom, and *D. coccinea* for its scarlet colour.

Cavanilles distributed seeds and tubers of his exciting new flower to botanic and university gardens in France, Italy, Switzerland and Britain. Diplomatic routes may also have played a part in their spread. The Marchioness of Bute, wife of the British Ambassador to Spain, is said to have sent seeds of *Dahlia coccinea* to the Royal Botanic Gardens at Kew in 1798, although the plants died. A few years later, in 1804, Lady Holland, wife of the British Ambassador in Madrid, received dahlias from Cavanilles which she sent back to Holland

House, where they produced double flowers in the care of the librarian before they also faded away. But she is credited with introducing dahlias to the UK and 20 years later, her husband sent her a note with the verse:

> The Dahlia you brought to our isle
> Your praises for ever shall speak:
> Mid gardens as sweet as your smile,
> And colour as bright as your cheek.

As more seeds and tubers arrived from Mexico, and more flowers appeared, the number of species identified by science grew. Far from the natural barriers of their native land, hybrids started to appear, aided by plant breeders on the one hand and an enthusiastic population of local insects on the other.

With species such as *Dahlia coccinea* variable in the first place, and the plant collections becoming hotbeds of interbreeding, planned and unplanned, the dahlias in cultivation started to become more and more diverse. This was exacerbated when breeders started actively selecting for characteristics such as colour and strong stems.

In 1805, a large consignment of plant material was sent by German naturalist Alexander von Humboldt to various key individuals in Europe, including to his mentor, Professor Carl Ludwig Willdenow. Willdenow decided to rename the genus *Dahlia* as the genus *Georgiana* after the German naturalist Johann Gottlieb Georgi. He went on to reclassify *Dahlia rosea* and *D. pinnata*, then considered distinct species, under the single new species name of *Georgiana variabilis*. This contributed to widespread taxonomic confusion and although Willdenow accepted the name *Dahlia* in 1810, *Georgiana* was used for several decades, particularly in Germany, and it regularly crops up in eastern Europe to this day.

By 1829, all the species in Europe were reclassified as *Dahlia variabilis*, but introductions, interbreeding and general confusion continued. In 1830 William Smith added the hypothesis that all dahlias could be divided according to colour – red-tinged or purple-tinged. This concept was expanded on by William Lawrence, a vigorous hybridizer of dahlias in the 1820s, who declared that the flowers could be assigned to one of two groups: Group I (ivory-magenta) or Group II (yellow-orange-scarlet). Things have been tidied up considerably in the last 200 years but disagreements persist.

Despite regional differences in dahlia classification, there are now well in excess of 57,000 cultivars which, wherever in the world they originated, are officially registered with the Royal Horticultural Society. These are listed in *The International Register of Dahlia Names, 1969*, which was reprinted in 1995 and is updated by annual supplements.

## The rise of the modern dahlia

In the early years of the nineteenth century, dahlias were a rich man's game. They were grown and tinkered with in the gardens of châteaux and large country houses, where there was time and money to cultivate both horticultural expertise and an academic interest in the new and intriguing. But tubers were expensive; hybrids that were exciting and fresh on the scene could command as much as £100 – several years' wages for a working man

– and even established cultivars would set the would-be enthusiast back as much as a guinea.

There was a touch of dahlia mania about the times. The flowers were all the rage and, in horticultural quarters at least, the talk of the town. Chance seedlings were pounced on for potential and, from the melting pot of species and hybrids, distinct forms started to emerge. Clean, straightforward Single dahlias were joined by a fully Double variety. Ball dahlias became popular and a smattering of Anemone forms emerged.

Attaining almost cult status, the first double-flowered cultivars were called Show and Fancy dahlias. The former were Ball-like and a single colour, while the latter were multi-coloured. Nurserymen and head gardeners were encouraged to experiment and to hybridize this exotic plant further, but it was the Great Exhibition held in London in 1851 that provided the stimulus for the explosion of colour and form that followed. Visitors from all walks of life saw dahlias for the first time and a huge love affair began.

The clamour for new varieties led to developments all over Europe. Collerette dahlias appeared in France, followed by Lilliput dahlias in Germany, a name that

## A Devilish Mystery

Despite their overwhelming popularity, Cactus dahlias didn't join the pantheon of cultivars until relatively late. The story goes that in 1872 a badly rotted shipment of dahlia seeds and plants was received by Mr J. T. van den Berg in Utrecht. Although it was unlikely that any of it would be viable, the nurseryman sifted through the slimy material and discovered a small piece of root that was still alive.

From this he grew a scarlet flower that was highly double, with petals rolled tightly backwards. This new form he called *Dahlia juarezii*, and when the plants were catalogued for sale in 1874, they caused a sensation. This remarkable discovery took dahlia breeding in a whole new direction and true Cactus dahlias – or *les étoiles du diable*, 'stars of the devil', as they are known in France – rapidly appeared. And, it is said that, because this mutation has not been discovered before or since, that tiny bit of root could be the ancestor of every Cactus dahlia in cultivation.

But the names and origins of plants provide no end of fun for those who seek it, and there is always someone who will shout 'Lies, damned lies!' and cite an alternative version of events. There are, therefore, those that claim that Cactus dahlias had a more prosaic origin, and that the first spiky double – promoted as a species – was really an early Mexican cultivar that arrived (possibly) via a nursery in France. Or that there may even be other instances of spiky flowers appearing, independently of *Dahlia juarezii*. There are also questions as to whether the plant material in the story was actually rotten or whether this detail romantically hijacks a similar tale of the discovery of the *Cattleya* orchid, which involved an almost magical resurrection of seemingly dead plant material by a talented and skilful horticultural wizard. But the first story, of the original Cactus dahlias overcoming adversity and near obliteration, is better.

the French amended to *pompone* for the resemblance to the bobble on the hats of their sailors. A revelation came with Cactus dahlias, their long, narrow petals rolled into tubes, that arrived, ostensibly at least, from Mexico. And a full-on tennis match of innovation and improvement between the Dutch and the Germans saw Peony dahlias give rise to Decorative dahlias, which were further bred and selected for ever more magnificent sizes.

An association with large, gaudy, showman's dahlias, and the somewhat obsessive attitude that comes with cultivating perfection, led to the genus falling into disfavour with gardeners and taste-makers as the twentieth century rolled on. Brash and blowsy was no longer the thing. The flower that was once so exciting and cherished was getting a resounding thumbs down.

But then came a renaissance. A new style of gardening emerged, more relaxed and informal, and with greater focus on containers. This was followed rapidly by a new sort of floristry, one where scent and colour, charisma and personality were key. The use of dahlias alongside other flowers and foliage to mute or enhance them, together with the arrival of varieties specially bred for cutting, revealed the flower to be every bit as desirable and exciting as it ever had been.

This change of attitude was bolstered by plants arising from a new crucible of dahlia breeding in New Zealand. A trip to Mexico in 1989 brought an epiphany for plantsman Dr Keith Hammett. He saw dahlia species growing in the wild, with elegant single flowers and highly diverse foliage, and changed the direction of his work. The result was a new twist on Collerette dahlias with collars darker than the outer petals, and the Mystic Series offering single flowers with a dark central disc and inky foliage.

# The genetic marvel

The genus *Dahlia* has around 36 species. A species is usually defined as a population of individuals which have a high level of genetic similarity and which can interbreed. Different species frequently arise because populations become separated by geographical barriers and the isolated groups evolve independently, developing unique characteristics. This appears to be the case with *Dahlia*. Most of the species have only limited ranges and are mainly found in Mexico; the exceptions are the widespread *Dahlia coccinea, D. australis,* which has a range that stretches into Guatemala, and *D. imperialis,* which occurs throughout Central America.

What often happens when plants are collected for horticulture is that individuals that might never ordinarily meet in the wild are put together in a garden setting and, with plenty of pollinators to aid the process, they interbreed promiscuously, creating all sorts of hitherto unseen variations.

In the case of dahlias, the fact that they are octoploid also contributes to diversity. This means that they have eight sets of chromosomes where most other plants (and humans) have just two. In addition to this, they have a lot of transposons. These are mobile pieces of genetic material that move from one place to another along the same chromosome or into a different one, altering the genetic make-up of an organism and creating or reversing mutations.

The huge mass of cultivated dahlias that are grown and loved all over the world derive from highly complex hybrids. The two main parents in formal hybridization are *Dahlia coccinea* and what is thought to be *D. pinnata* (although there is now doubt as to whether this is a true species), with others of the original 36 species that grow in Central America represented only sparingly. As discussed on page 19, this has resulted in difficulties in classification, in turn leading to cultivated dahlias being referred to as *Dahlia* × *variabilis*, or more recently *D.* × *hortensis* – the × referring to the fact that it is a hybrid, in this case often of unknown parentage.

The classification of dahlias is further hindered by the fact that morphological variation is highly pronounced within the genus. Due to the presence of transposons, they mutate spontaneously; in addition to which, they exhibit a significant degree of plasticity, where individuals of a dahlia cultivar grown under different conditions will look noticeably different.

Interestingly, the most recent leaps in dahlia breeding come from a combination of improved understanding of the genetics of the plant and from taking a fresh and scientific look at the wild populations, as pioneered by Dr Dayle Saar at Murray State University, Kentucky, USA. Dr Keith Hammett in New Zealand, meanwhile, has taken advantage of characteristics of less-utilized species such as *Dahlia dissecta* and *D. apiculata* to create new foliage effects to complement the flowers. His current breeding activities, in association with the University of Auckland, are bringing new varieties of tree dahlias to the market, introducing colours other than purple and white, and creating plants with solid woody stems.

## Colour magic

Dahlias come in the most fabulous array of colours imaginable – orange, pinks, whites and all combinations of the above; some even have a delightful burnished quality, as if dusted with gold. The only colours that are not represented are black (although some of the darkest reds give it their best shot) and true blue.

As with roses, which are similarly recalcitrant, there have been many unsuccessful attempts to breed a blue dahlia. In 1846 the Royal Caledonian Horticultural Society, based in Edinburgh, even offered a prize of £2,000 to the first person to do so, but the prize as yet remains unclaimed.

The problem all comes down to biochemistry. Anthocyanins are a family of pigment compounds that produce red, purple or blue colour in plants. They tend to be named after the plant in which they were discovered, so pelargonidin is bright red and discovered in pelargoniums, and delphinidin is bright blue – like delphiniums.

Dahlias contain anthocyanins and through various biochemical changes can express colours, up to and including dark red and purple. But delphinidin has six hydroxyl groups (a hydrogen and oxygen molecule) attached to the basic anthocyanin compound, made up of three rings of carbon molecules. Since dahlias have, so far, only produced five hydroxyl groups, that clear blue remains elusive.

But colour is a complex thing. Flowers are not art, with its combinations of primary colours and its shades, tones and tints; they are evolved biological systems. When light hits the pigments in the flower, it may be absorbed or reflected – and which wavelengths are absorbed and which are reflected depends on the precise combination of those pigments.

The colour that is perceived by any given individual is subjective and influenced by their neurological wiring, gender and experience. Furthermore, not only did these plant pigments evolve to signal to insects – who can see more wavelengths of light than gardeners – but they may change as the plant ages. An enormous number of physical influences can also affect plant colour, including the pH of the soil, underfeeding a plant or exposing it to a high level of UV light.

Therefore, while there have been numerous attempts to define dahlias (and other flowers) by colour, it is a blunt instrument at best. What colour is actually 'seen' depends on the conditions the plant is grown in, its age and genetics, in combination with the genetics, physiology and nervous system of the person looking at it.

So while nurseries, catalogues and authors make valiant attempts to do a flower justice, my shell-pink might be your soft lavender and where I admire a burgundy bloom, you might dislike its maroon overtones. Forgive me then, gentle reader, if what you see differs from my lyrical words. The truth is that colour descriptions can only be a guideline and photography can only go so far. And, as always, there is no substitute for experience, so go forth and grow.

## Anatomy of a dahlia

Dahlias are in the daisy family, the Asteraceae. This is a huge group of plants whose composite flower gave rise, in 1782, to the original family name of Compositae. Members range from the little yellow-and-white daisy that studs our lawns, to burdocks, thistles, knapweed, chicory, cornflowers, rudbeckias, asters, marigolds, dandelions, feverfew and chamomile.

Although the colourful bloom of a dahlia looks like a single flower, it is in fact an inflorescence. This is a cluster of tiny florets or individual flowers that sit within a receptacle; together making up the capitulum or flowerhead. There are two types of florets: disc florets, which resemble tiny tubes and make up the central hub, and a peripheral ring or rings of ray florets or ligulate florets. Each of these has a long, showy petal. The name 'ligulate' comes from the Latin *ligula* or 'strap'.

Dahlias grow from tubers that contain the storage carbohydrate inulin – the food that lets the plant grow away after winter dormancy. These tubers produce shoots at the crown that grow to form a bushy plant with hollow stems, bearing flowers at the top of each shoot. The flowers are usually arranged with a strong central bud and several smaller auxiliary buds.

**CROSS-SECTION OF A TYPICAL SINGLE DAHLIA INFLORESCENCE**

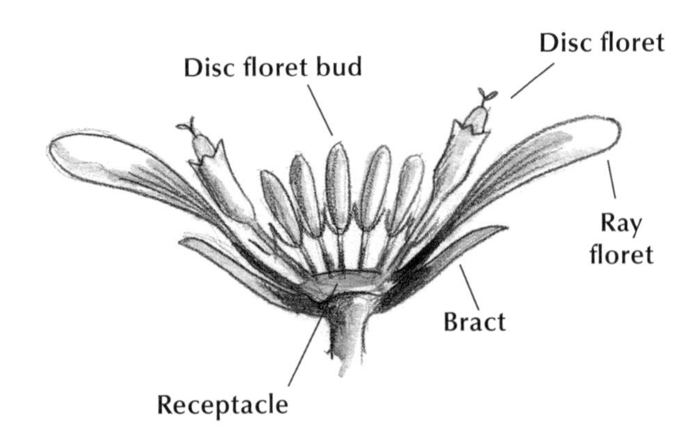


**DAHLIA TUBER**

# Dahlia classification

Classification presents certain challenges; there are tens of thousands of varieties, bred all over the world from the legions of hybrids and sports by hundreds of different growers. At the time of writing, not all dahlia societies are unanimous as to classification: the Royal Horticultural Society has 14 dahlia classifications and the American Dahlia Society has 21. Due to the diversity and plasticity of the genus, dahlias also represent an evolving landscape where there is still considerable academic research and debate.

In the domestic garden, however, there are really no wrong answers in this respect and this book includes four central chapters in which I have profiled a selection of varieties, chosen on the basis of their glamour, interest and charm, rather than official classifications. The way the plant is grown will make a difference to size but the average gardener is probably more interested in the way it looks. Indeed, the lines are often blurred as to where a particular cultivar does, should or might fall within the classification system.

Nonetheless, an understanding of dahlia organisation is valuable and the following is a summary of the main types and classifications that are broadly in use, drawing from the criteria set out by the Royal Horticultural Society in the UK and the American Dahlia Society. I hope it will help make sense of the terms and conventions used by local societies, dahlia nurseries and online retailers.

**DAHLIA STEM**
**Showing seedpod (a), flower (b) and bud (c)**

## SINGLE-FLOWERED

The simplest form of dahlia flower, this most resembles the true daisy family. It has a single row of petals, or ray florets, around a central hub of disc florets, and the flowers are often smaller than the more complex forms. The petals may be rounded, pointed or rolled, and the open flower form is very attractive to insect pollinators.

Sometimes used as dwarf bedding but also seen in full-sized plants, single dahlias are becoming increasingly popular and new varieties are being bred for small gardens and containers. These often have good foliage, too, with dark or finely cut leaves that provide a striking foil for the flowers.

## ANEMONE-FLOWERED

A relatively small group of dahlias, Anemones have one or two outer rings of petals, often flexed backwards towards the stem. The central boss of tubular disc florets, more prominent and less tightly packed than in other types, is quite large in proportion to the outer petals, giving the flower a fluffy, powder-puff appearance.

## COLLERETTE DAHLIAS

Fun and rather funky, these not-quite-single flowers appeared in France in the early days of dahlia breeding. They often have only eight or nine outer petals, but they have an additional, rather exotic, ruff of feathery petals around the central disc, and make good cut flowers.

## DECORATIVE

Glorious Decorative dahlias are softer in appearance than a Ball or Pompon dahlia (see pages 22–23), rounder than a Waterlily, and while less alarmingly dramatic than a Cactus type (see pages 22–23), they make up for it in their lusciousness.

A frothy mass of petals, these flowers are fully double with no central disc and they have strong stems, which makes them popular with florists and exhibitors. Each petal may be flat or slightly incurved but in some cases, such as Café au Lait and Labyrinth, they are twisted and rippled, giving the flower a relaxed and bohemian quality.

The term 'Decorative dahlias' covers a fairly large group of flowers. There are the enormous Dinner-Plate dahlias, huge, heavy and eye-catching, then there are those that are simply 'large', before you enter the world of ordinary-sized blooms. The size of the plant can vary enormously, too, from 2m (6½ft) giants to tiny, neat bedding dahlias, not much more than 30cm (12in) tall.

Within this classification, there are also Formal and Informal Decoratives, the difference primarily being the neatness of the flower. Formal dahlias have petals that are uniform and precise, with a crisp appearance; they show very well and act as a good focal point in a flower arrangement. Informal dahlias have softer, more crumpled petals, a bit as if the flower has just got out of bed. They make a relaxed addition to the garden, whether in borders or containers, and bring a romantic quality to arrangements.

## WATERLILY

This beautiful dahlia form is actually a type of Decorative Full Double, one with broad, regular petals that are flat or slightly curved, or occasionally, rolled inwards at the edges. The profile of the flower is flatter than most Double dahlias, saucer-like rather than rounded. While it cuts well for use in a vase, its resemblance to a waterlily is such that some people display it floating in a bowl of water instead.

SINGLE-FLOWERED
ANEMONE-FLOWERED
WATERLILY DAHLIA
COLLERETTE
DECORATIVE DAHLIA

## STELLAR

Stellar dahlias are another type of Decorative dahlia and can be defined as a separate category, too. Bold and dramatic, these have sharp, deeply cupped, crisply repeated petals that are swept back from the centre of the flower, giving it a toothed, dragon-scale quality that is really rather exciting.

## BALL AND POMPON

These dahlias are 'the round ones' of various sizes. They are neat, drumstick flowers made up of hundreds of tightly packed, semi-furled petals and are descended from the original Show and Fancy dahlias of the eighteenth and early nineteenth centuries.

Small Ball dahlias measure 10–15cm (4–6in), while Miniature Balls are up to 10cm (4in) in diameter. Pompon dahlias, meanwhile, are perfect tiny globes up to 5cm (2in) in diameter. Some cultivars span more than one category.

These floral lollipops may not have the silky, enveloping charms of an Informal Decorative or the sunny, bee-happy outlook of a Single, but they are a joy to an ordered mind. The tight twist of petals emerges from the centre in an expanding spiral, reflexing ever backwards to disappear towards the stem. Their show-bench heritage is clear and as a group, they are still popular with exhibitors, while florists find the erect stems and strong shape useful in arrangements.

## CACTUS AND SEMI-CACTUS

Cactus dahlias are some of the most exciting and dramatic dahlias on the market. Each fully double flowerhead is an explosion of pointy, punky petals, each one rolled backwards to form a tube. The flower form varies; it can be clean and sharp like a collection of sea urchins, or the petals may be reflexed or slightly curled, for a more sea-anemone – or alien-tentacle – effect.

Semi-Cactus is technically a separate group and visually these fall on a continuum between Cactus and Decorative dahlias – more soft in appearance, petals less tightly furled, but no less fun than Cactus types and with a similarly entertaining palette of colours.

Cactus and Semi-Cactus dahlias are good, versatile garden plants and the tight petals are less prone to damage by rain and wind than some plusher specimens.

## FIMBRIATED OR LACINIATED

Fimbriation describes the fringed end of a petal, divided as though snipped with scissors into a serpent's tongue or the frilly edge of a snowflake. Less a group of flowers and more of a characteristic, fimbriation, or laciniation as it is sometimes known, is particularly dramatic and exciting in Cactus and Semi-Cactus dahlias, but it can also be found in other types, including Decorative.

## MISCELLANEOUS

This section is used to describe dahlias whose formal classifications have now become disused and those that do not fall into the above groups. It is a bit of a shabby term, given that this includes the glorious Orchid and rather insane Double Orchid types, and and the now-no-longer-used (much) classification of Peony dahlias, as well as Fimbriated dahlias, Thistle dahlias and a number of other minor groups. This section also includes the species plants.

Single Orchid or Star dahlias (see page 24) have blooms with a single ring of petals around

STELLAR DAHLIA

CACTUS AND SEMI-CACTUS DAHLIA

BALL AND POMPON DAHLIA

FIMBRIATED OR LACINIATED DAHLIA

the disc. Resembling a pinwheel, the ray florets are curved either forwards or backwards at the edges. Double Orchid dahlias are fully double with no visible central disc.

Peony dahlias look rather like a single flower gone feral. While the Singles tend to be neat and fairly small, with just one row of flattened ray florets in the classic daisy style, the Peony types are still an open bloom but they double- or treble-up (or sometimes more) on the rows of petals. While some are neat, other varieties have lavish and voluptuous outer petals or petals near the disc that are twisted and curled.

# Societies and organizations

When dahlia mania struck in the mid-nineteenth century, it didn't take long for a competitive spirit to emerge among growers, and the National Dahlia Society was formed in Britain in 1881. Since then, dahlias have become wildly popular all over the world and there are collections and societies in Australia, New Zealand, the Netherlands, France, UK, Germany, and many other countries besides.

National societies hold a wealth of information about dahlia growing and suppliers in their corner of the world, and your nearest club or society should be your first port of call if you want to exhibit your dahlias. Societies may also list regional clubs and celebrate their achievements, shows and dahlia trials on the national stage. If you want to find out more or meet other dahlia lovers, your local club is a great place to start.

# Expert tips

In the UK, a good resource for unusual varieties is the National Dahlia Collection (nationaldahliacollection.co.uk). Established in 1983 in Oxfordshire, it was bought by Winchester Growers and moved to Varfell Farm near Penzance in Cornwall in 1998. The Dahlia Garden displays more than 1,600 varieties, old, new and as yet unnamed. You can visit free of charge and get up close and personal with more dahlias than you had ever imagined, or you can order rooted cuttings online.

See the website for details.

Other national societies include:

**UK:** dahlia-nds.co.uk

**USA:** dahlia.org

**New Zealand:** nzdahliasociety.50megs.com

**Australia:** dahliasaustralia.org.au

**France:** sfddahlia.free.fr

**Germany:** ddfgg.de

Dahliaworld.co.uk, though not a national society, is a phenomenal resource listing every dahlia cultivar registered and a huge number of suppliers and societies.

## Height and flower size

Dahlias are highly variable and while clearly some are bigger than others, the degree to which they are fed and watered has at least as big a part to play in the ultimate height that they will attain, as does their variety.

They are classified by form rather than height, but with smaller varieties there is a bit of a twist to this as height (or lack of it) is one of their key characteristics. With a certain amount of leeway when it comes to Series (which might not all be equal in height), it is generally accepted that a dwarf dahlia is one that does not exceed 60cm (24in).

There are some really dinky dahlias out there. Some of the shortest are Lilliput or

Mignon dahlias, which grow to no bigger than about 30cm (12in), but even these seem beefy next to the ultra-small Dahliettas, which come in at a mere 20cm (8in) and really leave one no excuse not to experiment with table containers and window boxes.

The Dwarf bedding dahlias are a little larger but still do not exceed 60cm (24in) tall. Gallery dahlias (see pages 102–103) are a relatively new group that is particularly valuable for pots or small gardens as they have substantial flowers on a relatively small plant, 30–50cm (12–20in) tall.

As is the case with the plants, flower size can vary considerably. And if you disbud a dahlia – removing the secondary flowers – the apical flower can become relatively huge. The quoted flower sizes are mainly those from the British National Dahlia Collection.

For reference, the flower sizes are measured as follows:
**Giant or Dinner-Plate dahlias, US AA size:** over 25cm (10in).
**Large dahlias, US A size:** 20–25cm (8–10in)
**Medium dahlias, US B size:** 15–20cm (6–8in)
**Small dahlias, US BB size:** 10–15cm (4–6in)
**Miniature dahlias, US M size:** up to 10cm (4in)

Sometimes number codes and abbreviations are used as shorthand in dahlia descriptions. For a key to this, it is best to refer to the dahlia society of the area or country in question.

## Dahlias as cut flowers

Dahlias make fantastic cut flowers and while they may not be particularly long-lasting, they are glorious. Some varieties, such as those in the Karma Series, are bred specifically for cutting, but other cultivars have similar natural advantages of long stems and good staying power, so it is worth experimenting. Consider cutting the flowers as a particularly efficient and enjoyable form of deadheading, as the more you cut, the more will grow. While you can disbud dahlias for large exhibition blooms, floristry often works the other way around, taking off the large and heavy central flower to encourage the smaller, more dainty blooms produced by the side shoots. Dahlias don't open well if cut in bud, so wait until they are almost fully open, and harvest while the flower is still very fresh and the back petals firm and waxy. Cut dahlias early in the morning when the air is cool and the cells of the plant are as turgid as possible. Put the flowers straight into a bucket of clean water as they will rapidly wilt if left languishing in a basket. When you are arranging them, trim the end of the stem again, under water, to prevent an air bubble forming that might block the uptake of water. These are thirsty plants and they will make vase water grubby if they just sit there, so refresh the water often to keep them going, cutting a little bit off the base of the stem each time. In hot weather, a tiny drop of bleach or white vinegar mixed into the water will slow bacterial growth and help make the flowers last longer.

# ROMANTIC

# Doris Bacon

Pretty Doris Bacon has a level of subtlety and romance that Ball dahlias sometimes lack. The tips of the tightly furled petals are white, bleeding into a sweet, pinkish mauve berry crush towards the base and where the edge of the furled floret faces into the flower.

An attractive garden plant, Doris Bacon is delightful used in wedding flowers, perhaps with *Penstemon* 'Raven' and white-and-pink daisies – try *Cosmos* 'Sweet Sixteen' – or, in high summer, with fragrant sweet peas such as 'Promise' and 'Prima Ballerina'.

---

**Flower type:** Miniature Ball
**Average height:** 100–120cm (40–48in)
**Average spread:** 70cm (28in)
**Flower size:** 5–10cm (2–4in)
**Foliage:** Green
**Staking:** A good idea when the plants are well grown
**As a cut flower:** Looks lovely as part of a bouquet
**In the garden:** Blends well with berry and cream colours
**Alternative varieties:** The Decorative dahlias Edinburgh and Duet, which is a dark red version, are similarly bicoloured, as are the juicy blooms of Mrs McDonald Quill

# Sierra Glow

This flower is a supermodel of the dahlia world. Tall, elegant plants with long, strong stems carry blooms of the most gorgeous bronze, brushed with coppery pink and with hints of dusty rose. It is a very plush creature indeed, glossy and polished, with its huge, richly petalled flowers the epitome of desirability and the very height of fashion.

In the garden, it's a stunner partnered with blue agapanthus or tall, tawny grasses. Cut this dahlia liberally and use as single stems in lavish, single-variety bouquets or as a striking addition to mixed arrangements.

---

**Flower type:** Large Decorative
**Average height:** 150–180cm (60–72in)
**Average spread:** 70cm (28in)
**Flower size:** 20–25cm (8–10in)
**Foliage:** Green
**Staking:** Yes, essential
**As a cut flower:** Elegant and sophisticated
**In the garden:** A beautiful addition
**Alternative varieties:** Café au Lait is a creamier version and just as glamorous, while Labyrinth is less cool in colour

# Worton Blue Streak

This is one of those optimistically named dahlias that is really more amethyst or lavender than it is blue, but it is a good flower nonetheless.

Emerging from plump green buds, the lilac blooms are fairly loosely furled by the standards of Semi-Cactus dahlias and, from certain angles, Worton Blue Streak could be mistaken for a Decorative dahlia. But on closer inspection, the edges of the petals do indeed recurve (bend backwards) along their length.

The flowers are relatively modest in size and the pleasing colour makes them an adaptable garden plant. They are versatile in floral arrangements, too.

Grow alongside white and pink cleome, mauve monarda or with dark blue *Salvia* 'Indigo Spires'.

---

**Flower type:** Small Semi-Cactus
**Average height:** 80–100cm (32–40in)
**Average spread:** 50cm (20in)
**Flower size:** 10–15cm (4–6in)
**Foliage:** Green
**Staking:** You'll probably get away without
**As a cut flower:** Lovely in a vase or bouquet
**In the garden:** A super dahlia and makes a good focal point
**Alternative varieties:** Decorative Hugs and Kisses has petals that roll forward, while loose Lavender Chiffon is a Semi-Cactus, but larger and blended with white

# Eveline

Romantic and ethereal, this lavender-flushed bloom recalls milky dawn mists over a late-summer meadow. Delicate, innocent prettiness, rather than a brash explosion of colour.

The green buds open to reveal mauve, but this disperses as the flower expands into glossy white petals with a hint of green at the base, while the younger, more coloured, petals form a distinct eye in the centre of the bloom.

Suitable for any use you can possibly imagine, Eveline is as elegant and classy as dahlias come – a silk flower reinvented in living perfection.

---

**Flower type:** Small Decorative
**Average height:** 120cm (48in)
**Average spread:** 60cm (24in)
**Flower size:** 15cm (6in)
**Foliage:** Fresh green
**Staking:** Yes
**As a cut flower:** Beautiful, particularly in white arrangements and bridal bouquets
**In the garden:** Pretty and delicate; good with other light-coloured flowers
**Alternative varieties:** Ryecroft Brenda T or Eternal Snow, which has a greenish tint to the centre, rather than purple

# Gerrie Hoek

The thing about gardening is that good performers persist. And the fact that Gerrie Hoek was introduced in 1942 and is still popular, pretty much tells us all we need to know. It is attractive, dependable and versatile, and is good both in the garden border and on the patio. The flowers are regular enough to hold their own on a show bench, while florists find that the strong, straight stems lend themselves to cutting.

The beautiful, prolific blooms are a classic Waterlily, held high on purple stems. The pointed petals are brushed a delicate shell-pink, and the chartreuse that is merely suggested at the tips is suffused at the base, which gives each bloom a greenish central glow and stops the flower appearing too sugary.

The plant is of medium size – large enough to make its presence felt – and nicely proportioned. The flowers, too, are just the right size; they have impact but are not so big that they flop. Gerrie Hoek looks lovely in the garden alongside gentle companions such as *Actaea simplex* 'Pink Spike', nicotiana and thalictrum.

---

**Flower type:** Waterlily
**Average height:** 100–130cm (40–52in)
**Average spread:** 60cm (24in)
**Flower size:** 10–15cm (4–6in)
**Foliage:** Green
**Staking:** Advised
**As a cut flower:** Lasts well in a vase or try floating it in a bowl of water
**In the garden:** Good, particularly in cottage-garden borders
**Alternative varieties:** Pearl of Heemstede, Wildwood Marie

# Crème de Cassis

This gorgeous little dahlia stops you in your tracks and is one of my absolute favourites.

Emerging from an inky purple bud, the upper surface of the petals is a pearly blackcurrant cream – hence this dahlia's name – while the back of the petal and the centre are a dark magenta-wine. The result is a beautiful bicolour effect of blackcurrant syrup poured over ice cream and given a bit of a swirl, and it also recalls the *sirop de cassis* that is one of the favourite drinks of Agatha Christie's famous fictional detective, Hercule Poirot.

The plant is not tall but the flowers are long-lasting and highly ornamental. It has strong stems for cutting and the flowers look fantastic with rich plums and dark pinks such as *Echinacea purpurea, Cuphea viscosissima, Verbena bonariensis* and asters (a genus now properly known as *Symphyotrichum*). Or try it with airy, lighter pinks, such as *Cosmos* 'Candy Stripe'.

---

**Flower type:** Small Decorative
**Average height:** 90–100cm (36–40in)
**Average spread:** 45cm (18in)
**Flower size:** 10–15cm (4–6in)
**Foliage:** Green
**Staking:** Not usually
**As a cut flower:** Good
**In the garden:** A really decorative, compact plant
**Alternative varieties:** Julie One and Crazy Legs have a similar two-toned effect but in orange, while Ferncliff Illusion and Razzle Dazzle are purple and white

# Café au Lait

If there was ever a dahlia that was made for a *House & Garden* photoshoot, then this is it. With sophisticated, billowing blooms as rich as a cream liqueur on ice, and with a subtle palette of nude shades that go with just about everything, Café au Lait is quite simply gorgeous.

Each bud opens to reveal a double flower, a multitude of pale pink petals that gradually fade to a warm cream-white, and with a blush of darker beige-peach in the centre. The flowers are lush, sumptuous and, growing up to 25cm (10in) across, they are eye-catchingly substantial.

Brides and florists love them and, while this is not a new variety, it is a strong contender for the dahlia *du jour* – everyone who is remotely serious about these things is growing Café au Lait and revelling in its softly stimulating charms.

---

**Flower type:** Large Decorative
**Average height:** 120cm (48in)
**Average spread:** 60cm (24in)
**Flower size:** 20–25cm (8–10in)
**Foliage:** Dark green
**Staking:** Benefits from staking
**As a cut flower:** Perfection in a vase
**In the garden:** Spectacular
**Alternative varieties:** Ice Cube, Shiloh Noelle, Sierra Glow

# Star Child

With a name that sounds as if it was conceived at a festival in the summer of love, and an appearance that borders on the ethereal, Star Child is a delicate Single dahlia with clear white petals and a bright gold central boss.

Bred in the USA in 1981, the name references its starry form – as is the case with a number of similar flowers in this group, including Natalie's Star, Juul's Allstar and Trelyn Seren – *seren* being the Welsh word for 'star'.

In the garden, Star Child is a pretty addition to planting schemes, fairly tall but not too large. And, like other Single dahlias, it is a useful source of late nectar for bees and butterflies.

---

**Flower type:** Single Orchid or Star
**Average height:** 120cm (48in)
**Average spread:** 60cm (24in)
**Flower size:** 10cm (4in)
**Foliage:** Green
**Staking:** Yes
**As a cut flower:** Excellent; a sweet and pretty addition to any arrangement
**In the garden:** Good; works well with grasses and airy foliage
**Alternative varieties:** Tahoma Hope, Juul's Allstar, Trelyn Seren

# Kelvin Floodlight

Kelvin Floodlight must surely be a contender for the largest dahlia around. The vast, buttery flowers are borne on a robust plant, giving an impressive display that turns up the temperature and illuminates the entire border.

But fine dahlia that it is, the name is something of a mystery. It is said in some quarters that the flower is named after Lord Kelvin, otherwise known as Sir William Thomson, who was a mathematician and physicist, and who became Professor of Natural Philosophy at Glasgow University in 1846 – a post he was to hold for more than 50 years.

In addition to giving his name to the Kelvin scale of heat measurement, he spent his career focussing on the practical utilization of science, and received his peerage for submarine telegraphy – solving the problem of laying telegraph cables under the Atlantic. His was also the first house in Glasgow to have electric lights, which leads us to a pleasing connection to floodlights and hence, potentially, to Kelvin Floodlight.

Yet the dahlia was introduced in 1958 in Australia, and 'Kelvin' was the prefix used by the breeder, a gentleman called Mr MacDougall, who also produced Kelvin Opal and Kelvin Rose, amongst others. So what link could there possibly be between MacDougall and Kelvin?

Back in Scotland, the little River Kelvin runs through the university area of Glasgow, where William Thomson worked and from which he took his name as a peer. And although MacDougall may or may not have been a fan of the learned peer, the name MacDougall has a distinctly Caledonian ring to it – so was he an expat Glaswegian perhaps? We may never know for sure.

---

**Flower type:** Giant Decorative
**Average height:** 80–120cm (32–48in)
**Average spread:** 40–50cm (16–20in)
**Flower size:** over 25cm (10in)
**Foliage:** Green
**Staking:** A good idea with such a big flower
**As a cut flower:** Good; pick while the flowers are very fresh
**In the garden:** High impact at the back of a border
**Alternative varieties:** Alva's Supreme, Bonaventure, Shirwell Greta

Series

# Happy Single

Brought to us by Dutch dahlia breeders Kees and Aad Verwer, the same people who introduced the Gallery Series of dahlias, the Happy Single Series is utterly delightful. At a height of 30–60cm (12–24in) and with spreads of 30–40cm (12–16in), they are versatile in smaller spaces and all have airy, finely cut dark foliage that provides a very fashionable foil for other plants.

As a collection, the Happy Singles – as they are fondly known – capture the richness of colour and simple joy of the single form. They have the exuberant look of a haphazard collection of seedlings, but careful breeding means that they achieve this apparently artless nirvana without the dud varieties that random genetic recombination inevitably brings.

The ever-increasing number of varieties includes Happy Single Flame, Happy Single Party, Happy Single Princess and Happy Single First Love. The petal colours vary, but they tend to bleed and intensify to a richly coloured halo around a contrasting central boss.

Perfect combined in borders or in a container collection, the open flowers are very attractive to butterflies and bees. Dwarf they may be but, in the garden, they are giants.

# Happy Single Wink

This is my personal favourite of the Happy Single Series. Compact plants with gorgeous deep bronze foliage produce a plethora of hot pink flowers, the petals of which deepen to claret towards the dark central boss.

I grow it in large ceramic containers, where, with plenty of food and water, it thrives. The thing I like about this arrangement is that it is super-versatile in my small garden. I can move the plants around to create edited highlights, and team them with other things, too, such as containers of cosmos and tubs of fuchsia. It keeps me entertained all summer long.

In the border, it is best near the front and works well with contrasting flowers such as bright blue or mauve salvias. Alternatively, try it in front of *Rudbeckia* 'Green Wizard' or apple-green *Moluccella laevis*.

Happy Single Wink received an Award of Garden Merit from the Royal Horticultural Society in 2012.

---

**Flower type:** Single
**Average height:** 50–60cm (20–24in)
**Average spread:** 40cm (16in)
**Flower size:** 5–10cm (2–4in)
**Foliage:** Dark and fabulous
**Staking:** Requires little or no support
**As a cut flower:** Good
**In the garden:** Superb at the front of the border and good in containers, too
**Alternative varieties:** There is a joyous collection of Happy Singles to choose from!

# Park Princess

Easy to grow, healthy and floriferous, this perky little dahlia is often seen in municipal planting schemes and massed bedding displays. Not all plants are suited to ultra-urban living, hordes of passing humanity and benign neglect, but Park Princess copes, excels even, bravely throwing out showy, weather-resistant flowers while she may.

The plant is sturdy and compact, flowering relatively early and keeping it up all season. The profusion of spidery flowers wins hearts and minds, while the dwarf size means that this dahlia works very well in pots and patio containers.

Introduced in the Netherlands in 1959, this princess may be small but she is a sweet and elegant addition to a garden. Try combining her with the fluffy tails of grasses such as *Pennisetum orientale* or with a small, deeper purple-coloured aster, such as 'Jenny'.

---

**Flower type:** Small Semi-Cactus
**Average height:** 60–90cm (24–36in)
**Average spread:** 30–60cm (12–24in)
**Flower size:** 10–15cm (4–6in)
**Foliage:** Green
**Staking:** No
**As a cut flower:** Good vase life
**In the garden:** Lovely, biddable front-of-border plant, and worth its weight in gold in pots
**Alternative varieties:** Pianella or, for a taller option, try Pink Preference

# Teesbrooke Audrey

A world away from the intense colours and enormous size of some of her brethren, Teesbrooke Audrey has a sweetly vintage quality. The flower is gently painted in delicate pastels, the petals are a soft lavender watercolour, and the feathered collar is white, with a hint of lilac at the tips.

This dahlia does not shout and scream and draw attention to herself, but she cuts well and looks lovely in an informal bunch, teamed with maroon and wine-coloured flowers. She is also beautiful and fitting in wedding and christening bouquets.

In the garden, the simple bloom is highly attractive to bees and butterflies, and combines prettily with airy *Verbena bonariensis* and with grasses.

---

**Flower type:** Collerette
**Average height:** 80–110cm (32–44in)
**Average spread:** 45–50cm (18–20in)
**Flower size:** 5–10cm (2–4in)
**Foliage:** Dark green
**Staking:** Advised but may get away without if well supported by neighbouring plants
**As a cut flower:** Excellent, particularly for weddings and christenings
**In the garden:** A charming border addition
**Alternative varieties:** Teesbrooke Redeye has a stronger pink colour, while Apple Blossom gives a similar effect but in yellow and pink

# Jomanda

There is something mesmerizing about Ball dahlias. Put them together in a vase and they capture the eye and play with your perception. The repetition of shape and form, the petals as they wax and wane in size, the delicate variations in colour. These all give a sense that you are in the presence of a fascinating puzzle that must somehow be decoded.

Raised in Holland by Cor Geerlings, who also introduced Cornel (see page 206), Jomanda is a lovely, autumnal caramel-pink colour with petals that reflex (see page 22) back to the stem. It received a Royal Horticultural Society Award of Garden Merit in 1998 and is an excellent all-rounder, performing well in the garden, as a cut flower and on the show bench.

Try growing it in the middle of a sunny sheltered border amongst shrubs, perennials and grasses. You may get away without staking Jomanda if it is grown in close company, otherwise, tie it in as the season goes on.

---

**Flower type:** Can be classified both as a Miniature Ball and a Small Ball
**Average height:** 100–120cm (40–48in)
**Average spread:** 70cm (28in)
**Flower size:** 7–10cm (3–4in)
**Foliage:** Green
**Staking:** Yes, in exposed places
**As a cut flower:** Excellent
**In the garden:** Bountiful Jomanda holds court in the autumn flower border, where its caramel tones go with everything
**Alternative varieties:** Minley Carol is a yellow-and-red blended pompon

# Inland Dynasty

If you are looking for a big dahlia, as in really big, then Inland Dynasty is one of the largest Semi-Cactus dahlias around. Fine plants with mighty stalks supporting splendid, juicy flowers that are as big as your head.

The brash, cheerful blooms are a sunny yellow colour and spiked like a punk's hairdo on a Saturday night. These beefy plants rapidly fill up the border with flowers, so grow them with grasses for a softening effect or team with hot colours and dark purples for a galaxy of exploding stars.

'Inland' is the prefix used by American dahlia breeder Norman Anselmo, who introduced Inland Dynasty in 1992.

---

**Flower type:** Giant Semi-Cactus
**Average height:** 120–180cm (48–72in)
**Average spread:** 90cm (36in)
**Flower size:** over 25cm (10in)
**Foliage:** Green
**Staking:** Yes
**As a cut flower:** Cut when the flowers are really fresh and the back petals still glossy
**In the garden:** A good back-of-the-border plant and impressive focal point
**Alternative varieties:** Clearview Sundance, Richard S

# Chilson's Pride

This is an unashamedly pretty dahlia. The blooms, clear pink with a creamy white centre, have a carefree, seaside feel. They speak of ice cream, beach huts and holidays. Each petal is slightly fimbriated (see page 22) and the relaxed feathering at the tips adds to the plant's informal quality.

Particularly popular in the USA, where it was introduced in 1954, Chilson's Pride is a good and versatile cut flower, and it lends itself to expressions of love and celebration.

Delicate and playful, an armful of these dahlias is the perfect way to rejoice in the arrival of a new baby. The sugary, Barbie-doll hues can be further sweetened with the addition of yellow and light blue. Or for a more grown-up love affair, give Chilson's Pride an edgier treatment by adding magenta and plum.

---

**Flower type:** Small Decorative
**Average height:** 90–120cm (36–48in)
**Average spread:** 100cm (40in)
**Flower size:** 10–15cm (4–6in)
**Foliage:** Green
**Staking:** Stake on an exposed site; in a decent mixed border you'll probably get away without
**As a cut flower:** Recommended
**In the garden:** Spectacular
**Alternative varieties:** Miracle Princess, Gerrie Hoek

# Thomas A. Edison

Bred in the USA and introduced in 1929, Thomas A. Edison has withstood every test that time and fashion can throw at it, and is still considered an outstanding cultivar – with good reason.

The rich, deep amethyst colour goes well with a huge number of other colours – pinks, whites, oranges and greens. It is beautiful and versatile in an ordinary herbaceous border with tall grasses and lush herbaceous planting, but it is also a cutting-garden heavyweight. As a cut flower it makes a lavish single-variety bunch but also mixes delightfully with smaller, more airy flowers, foliage and grasses.

Try it in the potager or ornamental veg patch, amongst green and purple kale and with dahlias David Howard and Jomanda. Include it in a tropical border with big-leafed bananas and cannas, or grow it in a pot and use it as part of a collection of containers – perhaps with houseplants such as palms and cheese plants that are spending summer in the garden – for a temporary display of exotica.

The dahlia is named for Thomas Alva Edison, the American inventor who is credited with the invention of the electric lightbulb. He also worked out how to record music and had 1,093 US patents registered in his name.

---

**Flower type:** Medium Decorative
**Average height:** 100–120cm (40–48in)
**Average spread:** 50–60cm (20–24in)
**Flower size:** 15–20cm (6–8in)
**Foliage:** Green
**Staking:** A good idea
**As a cut flower:** Excellent and versatile
**In the garden:** Mixes easily with other plants and looks fabulous at the back of a perennial border
**Alternative varieties:** Boogie Nites, Gonzo Grape, Purple Flame, Ripples

# Mystic Fantasy syn. Hawaiian Dreams

Dahlias have seen a revival in recent years, and this sea-change in opinion is, in no small part, due to the stylish new introductions from New Zealand plant breeder Dr Keith Hammett.

The Mystic Series (which has been rebranded and given new names for the American market, where they are increasingly available – hence the synonymous name) have fashionable deep purple-black foliage, like dark mahogany, which offsets the zingy flowers to perfection. They also have a compact, clumping habit, which makes them ideal for smaller gardens and containers, and renders stakes redundant.

Like its Mystic brethren, Mystic Fantasy has a neat single flower in a gorgeous blended cocktail of bright shades. It is a watercolour confection of peach, pink, apricot and rose, like a flock of flamingos at dawn. A delicate yellow halo bleeds into a puddle of raspberry crush around the dark central disc.

Strong contenders for my desert-island dahlia, Mystics add colour and pizzazz to tropical planting, and they are particularly good in small gardens and in containers.

---

**Flower type:** Single
**Average height:** 75cm (30in)
**Average spread:** 50cm (20in)
**Flower size:** 5–10cm (2–4in)
**Foliage:** Inky maroon
**Staking:** Compact plant, does not need staking
**As a cut flower:** Very pretty
**In the garden:** Flowers cheerfully all summer and is great in containers
**Alternative varieties:** Mystic Fantasy is part of a series of dahlias, of which Mystic Haze (syn. Dark Side of the Sun) has similar peach-pink tones

# L'Ancresse

For a simple, pure, classic dahlia, it is hard to beat L'Ancresse. Prolific and perfect, the white globes are borne on long, strong, straight stems so they float above the foliage of this relatively tall plant.

L'Ancresse is a place on the northern side of Guernsey in the Channel Islands, an area of pristine golden sands and turquoise sea. It is not known whether the name refers to an anchorage or a hermitage long-lost in time. However, it is rather appealing to associate this pristine dahlia with a life of monastic solitude and contemplation.

Despite being introduced in the 1980s, the virginal blooms have an antique quality, possessed of a formality and charm that lends itself to bridal bouquets. Whether bound tightly with white or blush rosebuds, or in a relaxed, modern arrangement with foliage and other white dahlias, L'Ancresse is simple and beautiful. Some flowers have a teasing hint of lilac that takes them just one step away from unapproachable purity and this makes them the perfect companions when walking down the aisle.

---

**Flower type:** Miniature Ball or Small Ball
**Average height:** 120cm (48in)
**Average spread:** 60cm (24in)
**Flower size:** to 10cm (4in)
**Foliage:** Green
**Staking:** Yes
**As a cut flower:** Long, strong, straight stems mean it is excellent for cutting and perfect for weddings and hand-tied bouquets
**In the garden:** Good
**Alternative varieties:** Boom Boom White, Eveline, White Aster

# FABULOUS AND FUNKY

# Summer Night

Crackling with dark energy and sultry romance, Summer Night reaches up out of the border and calls you with its siren song. It is a dahlia of passionate, moody demeanour, with long, narrow, pointed petals that bend back on themselves to form tight quills like a particularly spidery sea urchin.

The plant is sturdy and the stems are strong, so it makes a good and fashionable cut flower, as well as one that performs well in the garden. Summer Night is not to be confused with the similar-sounding Summer Nights or with Nuit d'Eté – the French translation of the same name, but, in reality, a different dahlia.

Plant it alongside *Verbena bonariensis* and orange zinnias or put it in a vase with pinks, plums and silvers – blush roses, purple physocarpus, copper beech, artemisia, sedums and eucalyptus, and seed pods and berries from around the garden – to celebrate the season.

---

**Flower type:** Medium Cactus
**Average height:** 120–140cm (48–56in)
**Average spread:** 50–80cm (20–32in)
**Flower size:** 15–20cm (6–8in)
**Foliage:** Green
**Staking:** Advised
**As a cut flower:** Lovely and dramatic
**In the garden:** Brings a compelling richness and intensity to a late-summer display
**Alternative varieties:** Chat Noir, Nuit d'Eté

# Roxy

Ravishing Roxy is a strong contender for the most sexy, sultry dahlia around. The flowers are a deep, glowing, magenta-pink, the tips of the petals are touched with lilac, and its maroon disc is freckled and rimmed with golden pollen.

A compact little thing, its pretty flowers are set off to perfection by alluringly dark foliage and the plant has a high-energy, dancing-queen quality that is perfect in the summer garden.

Pile cut blooms into a simple jug with harmonious pink, white and mauve flowers, such as cosmos, asters and sweet peas, and add herbs such as mint, feverfew and oregano for a relaxed, country-casual arrangement.

---

**Flower type:** Single
**Average height:** 50–70cm (20–28in)
**Average spread:** 30cm (12in)
**Flower size:** 5–7cm (2–3in)
**Foliage:** Blackish-green
**Staking:** No
**As a cut flower:** Puts on a good show
**In the garden:** An all-round stunner
**Alternative varieties:** Bishop of Canterbury is a little taller and Sweetheart is a little smaller

# Totally Tangerine

This charming little daisy has only been on the circuit a mere decade or so, but in that time, it has won ardent admirers right across the dahlia-growing world.

The plants are neat and compact, and the flowers have outer petals that are a soft pinkish orange on top (so not *totally* tangerine, in fact) and a deeper rose on the underside. The dense, fiery centre is made up of tiny tubular flowers with gold highlights at their throats, giving a kind of visual popping-candy effect.

Totally Tangerine is versatile, working well near the front of the border and lending itself to containers, too. It is also a cutting-garden stalwart. Try it in a bouquet with other orange and red flowers, such as fellow dahlias Darkarin and Chimborazo, and *Rudbeckia hirta* 'Cherry Brandy'. You can soften the arrangement with grasses and foliage if the sheer weight of flowers threatens to overwhelm.

---

**Flower type:** Anemone
**Average height:** 90cm (36in)
**Average spread:** 50cm (20in)
**Flower size:** approx. 7cm (3in)
**Foliage:** Green
**Staking:** Not necessary if you grow it with companions
**As a cut flower:** Good
**In the garden:** Great in the garden and a good compact plant for containers
**Alternative varieties:** Floorinoor, Ellen Huston

# Trelyn Rhiannon

Super-spiky Trelyn Rhiannon is really rather lovely. The petals are yellow at the base, morphing to pink at the tips and creating a gold heart surrounded by a pink neon haze – a forest of tight quills that makes the flower look positively fuzzy from a distance.

Punky yet charming, Trelyn Rhiannon adds colour to the garden in a series of controlled explosions. It is a versatile plant in both containers and borders and, while subtle it most certainly is not, it could be combined with other strong-shaped flowers to create a painterly scene – although the effect may be considered more Jackson Pollock than Monet.

When cut, the flowers are a fabulous and conceptual bunch of neon cacti, a frenzied paintball fight in a vase. Really, what's not to love?

Trelyn Rhiannon received a Royal Horticultural Society Award of Garden Merit in 2005.

---

**Flower type:** Small Cactus
**Average height:** 90–120cm (36–48in)
**Average spread:** 75cm (30in)
**Flower size:** 10–15cm (4–6in)
**Foliage:** Green
**Staking:** A good idea unless the site is sheltered
**As a cut flower:** Good
**In the garden:** Good
**Alternative varieties:** Tahiti Sunrise, Jessica

# Hot Cakes

Although some dahlias deport themselves perfectly normally, the genus does display a high degree of eccentricity. And of the more bizarre flowers that arise, the Anemone class are pretty bonkers, even by the standards of their contemporaries.

Hot Cakes is a case in point. The outer petals reflex towards the stem, thrusting the large and prominent penny bun in the centre of the flower upwards into your face, a giant caramel-orange powder puff dipped in gold dust that might just dab you on the nose. This centre is surrounded by a burnt raspberry corona that lightens towards the outermost tips of the petals and evolves gently as the flower matures.

And, it has to be said, there are madder Anemones still. Boogie Woogie looks rather as if someone has blow-dried a punk canary, while Mambo has a tangle of large, fimbriated (see page 22), purple-and-peroxide ray florets worthy of a Jon Bon Jovi vintage rock haircut. Which brings us neatly to Purple Haze, which is undecided as to where it sits. Known sometimes as 'variable', the swept-back shock of purple and pink is sometimes a classic Anemone type and sometimes more resembles a Peony. Like the best rock stars, it appears to be in a state of constant reinvention to keep us on our toes.

But to return to Hot Cakes. In the garden, the spicy hues and compact style of Hot Cakes work well with other orange and purple dahlias, and with soft, lime-green or plummy grasses, such as *Pennisetum* species. Experiment with it as a cut flower – purple kale or cotinus make a wonderful contrast – or mix it with airy fennel or wild carrot.

---

**Flower type:** Anemone
**Average height:** 100–150 (40–60in)
**Average spread:** 50–70cm (20–28in)
**Flower size:** 10cm (4in)
**Foliage:** Dark green
**Staking:** Advised
**As a cut flower:** Adds a taste of the unexpected
**In the garden:** A lovely spicy little number!
**Alternative varieties:** Rock Star, Topaz Puff

# Tartan

A bold berries-and-cream, Eton mess of a dahlia, Tartan really stands out from the crowd. It is huge. It is handsome. And with curling, swirling stripes of rich burgundy and snowy white, it is distinctly attention-seeking.

Although bred in New Zealand, Tartan is named for the Scottish cultural icon, its colours approximating to the hues of a claret or cherry tartan. This is a dahlia for those who are robust and fearless in their approach to garden design and who would rather channel their allegiance to warrior clans than listen to the buttoned-up taste police.

Use it in the garden with as rich and decadent a planting scheme as you can manage, or cut it to make an eye-catching floral centrepiece.

---

**Flower type:** Medium Decorative
**Average height:** 90–110cm (36–44in)
**Average spread:** 60cm (24in)
**Flower size:** 15–20cm (6–8in)
**Foliage:** Green
**Staking:** Advised
**As a cut flower:** Good
**In the garden:** Has a real wow factor
**Alternative varieties:** Other strong and uncompromising bicolour dahlias include the Cactus varieties Frigoulet and Piperoo, and the Informal Decorative Fuzzy Wuzzy, which has neatly snipped petals

# Platinum Blonde

There is something faintly suspicious about the idea of platinum blonde. A whiff of glamour that tries too hard, is too high-rent and has strayed from the path of pure perfection. A blonde who, with a slip of the bleach bottle, might become rather brassy.

Let us then pause to meditate on a natural beauty – a dahlia with outer petals of bleached ivory and a pronounced central pincushion of buttercream florets, each a tubular flower in its own right, offering its bounty to the passing wildlife.

This is no diva; this is a plant that is easy to grow and generous in its blooming. Delicate and sophisticated, it harks back to simpler times and eschews powder, paint and Photoshop in favour of unadulterated good looks.

Platinum Blonde is a sturdy plant that will be an asset in a white garden and alongside other pale dahlias such as Twyning's After Eight and the more delicate Star Child or Tahoma Hope. Or mix it into a border containing a range of seasonal plants and hues – blue agapanthus, white and pink cosmos, asters, eryngiums or the bold mauve spikes of liatris.

---

**Flower type:** Anemone
**Average height:** 120cm (48in)
**Average spread:** 50cm (20in)
**Flower size:** approx. 10cm (4in)
**Foliage:** Green
**Staking:** Preferably yes
**As a cut flower:** Good
**In the garden:** Great in borders and containers
**Alternative varieties:** Gitty Up is a similar shape but in rich orange and red, while Poodle Skirt is a hot pink-and-maroon version. Paso Doble continues the theme in lemon

# Hootenanny

In Scotland, a hootenanny is a party. It might be a festive get-together with singing and maybe dancing, or a spontaneous open-mic night with lots of people joining in to play folk music for the sheer pleasure of the thing. As Scottish settlers migrated to America, the word migrated with them. It also became used as a place-holding word for something momentarily forgotten, in the same way as one might use 'thingummy'.

But when it comes to the eponymous dahlia, a celebration is far more plausible than a mere thingummy. The outer petals are a luscious ring of cherry wine and the inner collar is a paler pink-violet, softly bleeding to white tips, like a fluffy feather boa draped around the dark bronze, pollen-laden central disc.

Introduced in 2005 and acquiring a Royal Horticultural Society Award of Garden Merit in 2015, this dahlia is also known as Hootenanny–Swan Island. The flowers are modestly sized and are ideal when grown in the border. Dancing with dark-leafed companions such as *Physocarpus opulifolius* 'Diabolo' or *P. opulifolius* 'Lady in Red', and with perhaps a touch of hot orange from zinnias or crocosmias, this dahlia is a party in its own right.

---

**Flower type:** Collerette
**Average height:** 120cm (48in)
**Average spread:** 50cm (20in)
**Flower size:** 10–15cm (4–6in)
**Foliage:** Dark green
**Staking:** Either stake or grow alongside supporting companions
**As a cut flower:** Great; cut when the flowers are open but young and fresh – the centre should still appear tight and waxy
**In the garden:** Good in borders and great in containers; very attractive to wildlife
**Alternative varieties:** Hillcrest Regal

Series
# Gallery

Dahlias are fabulous plants but they do have something of a reputation for being monsters. Great floriferous beasts made for mighty herbaceous schemes or robustly staked in rows for cutting and shows. Splendiferous, without a shadow of doubt, but not really a practical option for those of us with small gardens and balconies.

The gods of dahlia breeding are kind, however, and through extensive crossing of popular and attractive flowers with plants that are genetically predisposed to be small, over a period of about 15 years, they have produced the diminutive Gallery Series – which could come with the advertising tag, 'all the benefits of a real dahlia, only smaller'.

But, of course, they are real dahlias. Compact plants that grow between 30 and 50cm (12 and 20in) tall – with Gallery Art Fair on the more petite end and Gallery Art Deco a little larger. The fully double flowers – usually Decorative or Double Orchid types – come in a wide range of colours, appearing early in the season and continuing until the autumn frosts bite.

With more than 25 Gallery dahlias emerging since 1994, they are satisfying to grow, too. Excellent in containers and window boxes, they won't overwhelm even the smallest garden and are superb front-of-border plants in a larger one.

# Gallery Art Nouveau

With sweeping spirals of loosely quilled purple petals, the Double Orchid dahlia Gallery Art Nouveau has the classic good looks of its kind. It has a stylish two-tone effect – bright lilac on the upper side of the petals and a darker cherry-mauve underneath – rather like its parent, Gallery Art Deco, which displays the same effect but in orange.

At between 40 and 50cm (16 and 20in), Gallery Art Nouveau is at the taller end of the Gallery Series. It was honoured with a Royal Horticultural Society Award of Garden Merit in 1999.

---

**Flower type:** Double Orchid
**Average height:** 40–50cm (16–20in)
**Average spread:** 30–40cm (12–16in)
**Flower size:** 10–15cm (4–6in)
**Foliage:** Green
**Staking:** No
**As a cut flower:** Why cut it when you can have it in tubs, right where you can see it? But if you must snip the blooms, they perform well in a vase
**In the garden:** Perfect in pots and in small plots
**Alternative varieties:** Gallery Art Fair is a fresh white, Gallery Art Deco has a similar form and markings but in orange, while Gallery Rembrandt is a purple Decorative dahlia in the same Series

# Cheyenne

Kerpow! Blam! This is a completely unmissable flower. If Batman had a dahlia, it would probably be Cheyenne.

Selected in the USA in 1975, this dahlia is an action-packed vision of drama, with bright, feathered, flame-red petals that shoot out in all directions from a molten-gold heart. In the border or cutting garden, the flowers create a series of visual explosions, carroty fireballs of floral implausibility.

However, Cheyenne can also be grown in the veg patch, packed in between the sweetcorn and the leeks, bringing a buzz to the broad green leaves of scrambling squash plants, or offsetting beautiful purple and glaucous members of the cabbage family. In potager and border alike, the large, fuzzy flowers are particularly good teamed with other orange flowers such as marigolds, nasturtiums, gingery snapdragons and the dark-leafed dahlia, Moonfire.

---

**Flower type:** Fimbriated or Laciniated Medium Semi-Cactus
**Average height:** 100–150cm (40–60in)
**Average spread:** 80cm (32in)
**Flower size:** 15–20cm (6–8in)
**Foliage:** Mid-green
**Staking:** Not usually necessary
**As a cut flower:** Looks lively in a vase
**In the garden:** Spectacular in the border and will do well in a large tub as long as it gets plenty of water
**Alternative varieties:** Mel's Orange Marmalade, Terrie Bandey, Vuurvogel or Belle of the Ball, which is pink

# Alfred Grille

An exciting-looking dahlia that stands out from the crowd in a good way, Alfred Grille resembles something you'd find when diving off a coral reef – a pastel yellow sea anemone with soft pink tentacles waving gently in the currents – or, more exotic still, an alien life-form inhabiting your garden.

The flowers have a lovely form, with long, thin, inwardly curved petals on strong stems, and the plant is vigorous and easy to grow. And, while even the now-reformed, modern, dahlia-loving fashion police might describe it as a little bit gaudy, it is also dazzlingly joyful.

In a garden setting, the tight quills give the flower an airy quality, softening the colour scheme and helping it fit in remarkably well.

This explosion of floral fun was raised in Germany in 1965.

---

**Flower type:** Medium Semi-Cactus
**Average height:** 100cm–150 (40–60in)
**Average spread:** 45cm (18in)
**Flower size:** 15–20cm (6–8in)
**Foliage:** Green
**Staking:** Yes
**As a cut flower:** Excellent
**In the garden:** A joy to behold
**Alternative varieties:** Electric Flash

# Blue Bayou (syn. Bayou)

Originally just known as Bayou, the 'Blue' part of the name has crept into use as a happy but optimistic alliteration.

It is a striking plant, sporting showy reddish purple buds that open to reveal an Anemone flower with a berry-stained centre surrounded by petals of frosted blackberry ice cream. It is sultry and even slightly magical in appearance, but blue – clear, caerulean blue – it most certainly is not.

In 1952, a Mr H. F. Newsom, Secretary of the National Dahlia Society, was reported as declaring that there was a fortune waiting for the man who created the first blue dahlia. 'The Americans would go mad for it,' he said. But that dahlia has never been bred and the fortune has never been claimed.

Flower colour arises in a sequence of biochemical steps. The anthocyanin delphinidin – that gives flowers like delphiniums and violas their bright blue colour – requires six hydroxyl groups, but with only five, dahlias have not yet made the evolutionary grade. Breeders are working on this and have been for years, but although there are a number of dahlias with blue in their name, including Bonny Blue, Blue Beard and Blue Wish, in reality these are just ambitious shades of purple.

But purple is no bad thing. Resembling a giant mauve buttercup, Blue Bayou is vivid as part of an arrangement with dahlias such as Rip City, Karma Choc and Zirconia. Plant it in front of a stand of light green *Miscanthus sinensis* var. *condensatus* 'Cosmopolitan', or use it with clear orange flowers for a high-voltage display.

---

**Flower type:** Anemone
**Average height:** 100–150cm (40–60in)
**Average spread:** 50cm (20in)
**Flower size:** 7cm (3in)
**Foliage:** Green and leafy
**Staking:** Advised
**As a cut flower:** Very good
**In the garden:** Ideal – showy, free-flowering, and a magnet for butterflies and bees
**Alternative varieties:** Mambo, Purple Haze

# Crazy Legs

If your taste is for the unexpected and unusual, you could do worse than grow Crazy Legs. A form of Decorative dahlia that is often put into a class of its own – Stellar dahlias – the flowers are slightly flattened, with petals swept back, rather as if it is standing in a wind tunnel.

The colouring is intriguing, too. Like Crème de Cassis (see page 42), the petals are uniformly coloured but have contrasting shades top and bottom. This creates a striking two-tone effect – orange-bronze on top with russet-red underneath – which is visible as an accent, rather as one might flaunt the bright silk lining on a nice coat.

The flowers are prolific and are carried on long, strong stems. They are a splendiferous addition to autumn arrangements and look particularly good with red flowers, beech leaves, coloured cornus stems, and with berries and rosehips. They also perform in the garden, where they can flower over a long period and stand up pretty well to poor weather.

---

**Flower type:** In general, they are known as Stellar in the USA and Decorative in the UK
**Average height:** 90–120cm (36–48in)
**Average spread:** 80cm (32in)
**Flower size:** approx. 8cm (3½in)
**Foliage:** Green
**Staking:** Yes
**As a cut flower:** Really good, particularly in autumn arrangements
**In the garden:** Adds an interesting dimension to a mixed border
**Alternative varieties:** Gitts Crazy is a bigger version and Jescot Julie has similar colouring but in Double Orchid form. For a dwarf or container type, try Gallery Art Deco

# Optic Illusion

This rather snazzy cultivar was bred by Swan Island Dahlias in the USA in 1992. It is a curious creature; each rounded, rose-purple, wine-tinged petal is doubled up with a smaller white petaloid. This gives a lush and feathery bicolour effect. But it does make you wonder if your eyes are working properly or whether you might be seeing double.

Perhaps the name is toying with us; perhaps it is less an optical illusion to confuse the eyes, more a punning play on optics – those dispensers of strong drink that might make us see pink elephants, let alone pink dahlias.

But although the flower has the reputation of being variable, Optic Illusion is a dramatic and handsome addition to the garden, where it can be anchored with plush purples like *Lysimachia atropurpurea* 'Beaujolais' and the dark leaves and flowers of *Physocarpus opulifolius* 'Diabolo' and *Penstemon* 'Raven'. Alternatively, let it go wild with orange chrysanthemums, *Lychnis coronaria*, and hot pink asters and lilies.

---

**Flower type:** Small Decorative (sometimes described as Novelty)
**Average height:** 90–120cm (36–48in)
**Average spread:** 70cm (28in)
**Flower size:** 10–15cm (4–6in)
**Foliage:** Green
**Staking:** Preferred
**As a cut flower:** Very good
**In the garden:** Holds its own in the border
**Alternative varieties:** Audacity has not dissimilar colouring, while Caribbean Fantasy also provides a taste of the unusual

# Caribbean Fantasy

Bringing the party off the beach and into the garden, Caribbean Fantasy arrives with a whiff of bright cocktails, a dash of rum punch and a lazy reggae soundtrack. The burgundy-streaked petals blend from white to golden at the base, creating a heart of sunshine that pulls you in and makes you dream of silver sand and sapphire seas.

Tricolour dahlias are relatively unusual, even in the crazy mutated world of the genus, but here, the hot, tropical hues deepen as the flower matures, becoming richer and more compelling. This gives Caribbean Fantasy an even more exotic feel and, although the sun may not be setting across an island paradise, the flower keeps the holiday dream alive.

---

**Flower type:** Small Decorative
**Average height:** 100–150cm (40–60in)
**Average spread:** 75–90cm (30–36in)
**Flower size:** 10–15cm (4–6in)
**Foliage:** Green
**Staking:** Not usually necessary
**As a cut flower:** Very good
**In the garden:** An exotic and unusual talking point
**Alternative varieties:** Peaches and Cream is another tricolour dahlia

# Nijinsky

Nijinsky is a classic Ball dahlia in a cheerful, glowing pink-mauve colour that sits well alongside other garden plants.

The pattern of cell division in this flower follows the Fibonacci sequence, where each number is the sum of the two that precede it, so you get 1, 1, 2, 3, 5, 8, 13, 21, and so on. This gives rise to 'the golden spiral' that underpins the pattern that you see in pineapples, the arrangement of bracts on a pine cone and the unfurling crozier of a fern. The arrangement of ray florets on a Ball dahlia is a perfect example of the Fibonacci sequence working in a natural setting.

But mathematical pedigree aside, this is a very pretty flower. The violet baubles like funky purple tennis balls bounce the eye around the garden, while the cut flower works well in combination with blousy blossoms and muted hues, such as late-season hydrangea heads or pink roses, calla lilies and phlox.

---

**Flower type:** Small Ball
**Average height:** 90–120cm (36–48in)
**Average spread:** 70cm (28in)
**Flower size:** 10–15cm (4–6in)
**Foliage:** Green
**Staking:** Preferred, unless grown through other plants
**As a cut flower:** Very good
**In the garden:** Very good, versatile flower
**Alternative varieties:** Aurora's Kiss, Hamari Rose, Westerton Folly

# Neon Splendor

Introduced by Swan Island Dahlias in the USA some time prior to 1987, this brilliant flame-orange dahlia is all bright-lights-big-city, and brings energy and fire to any party.

It is the floral equivalent of heading down to Soho on a Thursday night, finishing dinner with Grand Marnier on ice, then downing a couple of peach schnapps shots before heading to Theatreland to continue the party. Cheeky, riotous and slightly decadent, to be sure, but it's London, Paris or New York neon, rather than Las Vegas.

Grow it with plants that are equally splendiferous – the smaller sunflowers, delphiniums, *Amaranthus caudatus* or *Leycesteria formosa*. Or, for glaucous greens and blues, try it with tall, structural *Onopordum* or in front of exotically cool *Melianthus major*.

After all, this glamorous dahlia may be bright, decorative and inclined to live life to the full, but it is classy, darling, always classy.

---

**Flower type:** Medium Decorative
**Average height:** 100–120cm (40–48in)
**Average spread:** 60cm (24in)
**Flower size:** 15–20cm (6–8in)
**Foliage:** Green
**Staking:** Advised
**As a cut flower:** Adds impact to autumn arrangements
**In the garden:** The life and soul of the party
**Alternative varieties:** Mrs Eileen, Parkland Glory, Motto

# DRAMATIC AND DARING

# Hamari Gold

The stuff of gardening dreams, Hamari Gold is a huge and glorious flower. The long, soft, gently frilled petals are a rich, glossy butter colour with a burnished metallic sheen that glows gently in the sun. The juicy great buds expand to reveal petals that begin life quilled and then flatten out as they mature.

Hamari Gold makes an impressive garden plant and is a good all-round performer as a cut flower and, when restricted, for showing. Introduced in 1984, it was awarded a Royal Horticultural Society Award of Garden Merit in 1993.

---

**Flower Type:** Giant Decorative
**Average height:** 100–130cm (40–52in)
**Average spread:** 80cm (30in)
**Flower size:** over 25cm (10in)
**Foliage:** Green
**Staking:** Advised, as the flowers are heavy, particularly when wet
**As a cut flower:** Make sure you cut when the petals at the back of the flower are still fresh and glossy
**In the garden:** Goes well with most things!
**Alternative varieties:** Bonaventure, Go American, Fairway Pilot

# Black Narcissus

Black Narcissus is a tall plant smothered in slightly implausible, dark red sea urchins. Raised in the mid-1950s in Canada, the fimbriated petals jut out in all directions, dramatically starry and softly fringed.

The flowers are gorgeous in autumn bouquets with copper-beech leaves and bronze dahlias of a contrasting form, or teamed harmoniously with pink, rose and cream flowers. In the garden, they will form a marvellous mixed display with other tall plants like delphiniums and sunflowers.

Naming plants, especially plants as diverse, wild and whacky as dahlias, is notoriously arbitrary. It is generally thought that Black Narcissus was named for the 1947 film but the reason for this choice, if, indeed, there was any reason other than that the breeder liked it, appears to have been forgotten.

---

**Flower type:** Medium Cactus
**Average height:** 120–180cm (48–72in)
**Average spread:** 100cm (40in)
**Flower size:** 15–20cm (6–8in)
**Foliage:** Green
**Staking:** Yes
**As a cut flower:** Good; cut when about three-quarters open to prolong vase life
**In the garden:** An attention-grabbing plant!
**Alternative varieties:** Nuit d'Eté, Summer Night

# Checkers

I am rather ambivalent about this dahlia. The modestly sized flowers are striking; dark red with offset white ovals or diamonds on the ends of the petals that give the flower a chessboard quality. A bold look, certainly, but do I like it? I am not sure.

Introduced by Gitts in the USA in 2001, Checkers is startling, almost unreal – or perhaps the flowers are in the midst of a transformation. It brings to mind *Alice in Wonderland*, when Alice stumbles across the royal gardeners painting the white roses red, because if the Queen of Hearts discovers they are the wrong colour, she will chop the gardeners' heads off.

With the base of the flower richly daubed with a colour that might be called Redcurrant Delight, or some similar hue, and the tips still in matt white emulsion, there is a sense that some literary gardener, painting the roses red, might have been alarmed away during his task.

But ... As the Queen of Hearts herself declares, 'Who dares to taint, with vulgar paint/ The royal flower bed?' Well, quite.

---

**Flower type:** Miniature Decorative
**Average height:** 90–110cm (36–44in)
**Average spread:** 30cm (12in)
**Flower size:** up to 10cm (4in)
**Foliage:** Green
**Staking:** You may well get away without
**As a cut flower:** Good
**In the garden:** A striking addition
**Alternative varieties:** Duet or Aitara Diadem; Jamaica has red-and-white striped petals

# Rip City

With compelling good looks, this black-crimson dahlia has stolen a lot of hearts in its time and when you see it in the garden on an early autumn morning, a symphony of rich, ruffled, berry colours, darkest in the centre and fading to magenta as the petals age, it is easy to see why.

The name Rip City is a nickname for Portland, Oregon, in the north-west of the USA, and is specifically associated with the National Basketball Association team, the Portland Trail Blazers. In 1971, the Blazers were up against powerful adversaries when a wildly ill-advised long shot dramatically went home. In the heat of the moment, the announcer shouted 'Rip City! All right!' – and the name stuck.

And when it comes to drama, Rip City does not sell the crowds short. Vigorous and lush in growth, the fully double flowers have petals that recurve for more than half of their length, giving the bloom a slightly louche appearance.

---

**Flower type:** Small Semi-Cactus (sometimes sold as an Informal Decorative)
**Average height:** 100–110cm (40–44in)
**Average spread:** 80cm (32in)
**Flower size:** 10–15cm (4–6in)
**Foliage:** Dark green
**Staking:** Ideally
**As a cut flower:** Good
**In the garden:** Fantastic and dramatic
**Alternative varieties:** Chat Noir, Orfeo

# Magenta Star

This magnificent magenta monster is a towering addition to a mixed border. It looks fabulous alongside tall, airy grasses and frondy fennel, or against harmonious plummy *Eupatorium*. Alternatively, go for neon brights, mixing it up with tall yellow daisies like *Rudbeckia maxima*, and orange cannas and crocosmias.

The brilliant pink flowers of Magenta Star have a dark red central boss fringed with gold anthers. They are carried over foliage that is finely divided and an unusual greenish-purple-black hue, a little like damp Welsh slate.

Adored by bees and butterflies, and winner of a Royal Horticultural Society Award of Garden Merit in 2008, Magenta Star provides a splendid crescendo to late summer and early autumn. To be sure, it is a beast of a plant but what a very handsome beast it is!

---

**Flower Type:** Single
**Average height:** 130–150cm (52–60in)
**Average spread:** 60cm (24in)
**Flower size:** 5–10cm (2–4in)
**Foliage:** Purple-black
**Staking:** Yes, very necessary
**As a cut flower:** Lovely – as dramatic in the vase as it is in the border
**Alternative varieties:** Try Bishop of Canterbury for a smaller and more muted magenta dahlia, or Roxy for something smaller still

# Pooh

Back in 1924, artist E. H. Shepherd illustrated a short series of books featuring Christopher Robin and his stuffed-with-fluff teddy bear, Winnie-the-Pooh. Why Pooh? Because 'pooh' was the sound that he made when blowing a fly off his nose. But I digress.

Even in the early versions of the book, Pooh Bear occasionally wore a jacket and, when the books were printed in colour, it was a red one. So, although the world is no longer black and white, and the line drawings have morphed into animation and Disney ubiquity, the bear himself got bolder (if not necessarily brighter), as the years went by.

Given that Pooh is attractive to bees and bees make honey, one could imagine that The Bear Himself would be quite pleased about his eponymous dahlia. With dark orange petals dipped in custard at the tips, and a handsome golden ruff in the centre, it is the perfect floral embodiment of the bright yellow bear and his red jacket – cheerful, childlike and paint-box fresh.

As Pooh–Swan Island, this dahlia won a Royal Horticultural Society Award of Garden Merit in 2009, and has proven itself an excellent garden plant. The flowers are shapely and produced prolifically, and it is a great addition to a late-summer border.

---

**Flower type:** Collerette
**Average height:** 90–120cm (36–48in)
**Average spread:** 60cm (24in)
**Flower size:** 8–10cm (3½–4in)
**Foliage:** Green
**Staking:** Advised
**As a cut flower:** Good
**In the garden:** Cheerful and versatile
**Alternative varieties:** Fashion Monger is red and white, while Impression Fabula is an interesting purple version

# Zorro

This giant, blood-red Decorative dahlia is named after the fictional, Robin Hood-like hero Don Diego de la Vega, who assumes a secret identity as Zorro – Spanish for 'fox'.

A dashing, black-clad, masked outlaw, he protects the common people from tyrannical but bumbling officials. The story has been retold many times on stage and screen but it was particularly popular in 1987, when this dahlia was raised.

A true garden swashbuckler, the flowers of Zorro are big and showy with deliciously ruffled red petals. Cutting a dash in the border, it received an Award of Garden Merit from the Royal Horticultural Society in 1995.

In the garden, put it where it will blend with the autumn colours as they develop – near maples or liquidambar, or in front of crab apple trees and berried plants. As earlier-flowering plants start to develop their seed heads, Zorro will keep the floral quotient high and vibrant, and maintain a sense of freshness.

---

**Flower type:** Giant Decorative
**Average height:** 130–150cm (52–60in)
**Average spread:** 50–75cm (20–30in)
**Flower size:** over 25cm (10in)
**Foliage:** Green
**Staking:** Yes – the heavy flowers need the support
**As a cut flower:** Good
**In the garden:** Makes a splash
**Alternative varieties:** Sam Hopkins, Rip City, Spartacus

# Moonfire

A fantastically eye-catching dwarf bedding dahlia, Moonfire lives up to its name. Golden orange flowers blend sharply to vermillion at the base of the petals and the dark chocolate central disc is fringed with arrestingly bright pollen. These psychedelic harvest moons are sprinkled liberally over a night sky of foliage that is the deepest, blackest mahogany-plum.

Received in error for another cultivar by Bridgemere Nurseries in the UK, the seedling was named by Chris Sanders and honoured with an RHS Award of Garden Merit in 1998. But in an unexpected plot-twist, on a trip to a Dutch dahlia trial ground the nurseryman saw his delightful Moonfire labelled as Sunshine. And there was a further problem. The International Dahlia Register has three instances of the name Sunshine, all with inadequate data, and it was not possible to definitively link Moonfire to any of them. Fortunately, the-plant-widely-known-as-Moonfire was never actually distributed as Sunshine, and the International Cultivar Registration Authority proposes to formally sanction the epithet Moonfire, which should tidy things up nicely.

Whatever its name, this is a dinky little dahlia with many assets. It is easy to grow and good for beginners, while its open flower form makes it a valuable source of nectar for bees and butterflies. It excels as a border plant, where it can be teamed with other orange and red flowers. It looks great alongside crocosmia varieties such as 'Lucifer' or 'Star of the East' and with rudbeckia or red-hot pokers such as *Kniphofia* 'Royal Standard' that have similar hues but a contrasting form. Alternatively, try it with hot pinks; dark sedums and bold echinaceas set it off a treat.

---

**Flower type:** Single
**Average height:** 70cm (28in)
**Average spread:** 40cm (16in)
**Flower size:** 5–10cm (2–4in)
**Foliage:** Dark bronze
**Staking:** No
**As a cut flower:** Puts on a decent show
**In the garden:** Wonderful in the border and perfect in patio pots
**Alternative varieties:** Happy Single Flame, Ian Hislop

# *Dahlia coccinea*

The species *Dahlia coccinea* is widespread and fairly common in its native Mexico. As one of the earliest arrivals in Europe, it was widely used in hybridization and so is the ancestor of many of today's cultivated dahlias. It is quite variable in both size and colour, though *coccinea*, from the Latin meaning 'scarlet' (the same root word as cochineal, a colouring derived from a beetle), implies that the flower is red.

The species has a number of forms. The popular *Dahlia coccinea* var. *palmeri* is a large plant that can vary a lot but has been known to reach 180cm (72in). However, it wears its size lightly: its foliage is finely divided and airy, and its cheerful little orange daisies sprawl and scatter through a border, providing a lot of pleasure for very little fuss.

The variety pictured here goes by both *Dahlia coccinea* 'Great Dixter' and *D. coccinea* 'Mary Keen', named after the well-known garden designer and writer. It is a good example of how plants end up with two names. The National Dahlia Collection (NDC) was gifted a form of *coccinea* many years ago from Great Dixter – home and garden of the great dahlia lover Christopher Lloyd. As it was apparently unnamed, they called it *D. coccinea* 'Great Dixter' and proceeded to show and market it accordingly.

Ages later, Mike Mann of the NDC met Mary Keen looking at dahlias at the Royal Horticultural Society's Chelsea Flower show, when she pointed at one labelled *D. coccinea* 'Great Dixter' and exclaimed, 'Isn't that "Mary Keen"?'

Discussion ensued and they concluded that the plant was one and the same. So the names are synonymous and you may find it sold under either.

---

**Flower type:** Species with single flowers
**Average height:** 100–120cm (40–48in)
**Average spread:** 70cm (28in)
**Flower size:** 10cm (4in)
**Foliage:** Green
**Staking:** No, let her ramble through the border
**In the garden:** Lovely when grown through other plants
**As a cut flower:** Good
**Alternative varieties:** *Dahlia coccinea* is variable and various forms are available

# Arabian Night

The name of this dahlia cultivar comes from the *Arabian Nights* – or *One Thousand and One Nights*, as it was originally called in Arabic. This is a compilation of stories, and stories within stories, collected over many years from Persian, Egyptian and Indian folklore and literature.

In the first and framing story, which encompasses the rest, King Shahryãr was betrayed by his unfaithful wife, so he had her executed. Then, despairing of the fidelity of womankind, he developed the somewhat bitter habit of marrying virgins and executing them the following morning.

When the kingdom ran out of virgins, the Vizier's daughter, Scheherazade, offered herself as wife to the king. But she had a plan. Each night she would start to tell him a story but would stop at a critical point, leaving the king keen to know what happened. The following night she would start another tale but not finish it, and so on. In the end, he decides not to execute her and they live happily ever after.

It is hard to know whether this lush, deep claret dahlia is named for the sumptuous velvets that must surely bedeck a royal bedchamber, or whether it is that it is fit to distract a murderous king. But in either case, the flowers are prolific and captivating. It is charming in bouquets and eye-catching in gardens, where it looks particularly lovely planted against a white or pale blue wall, or with fresh green companions such as *Moluccella laevis* to pick up the contrasting green floral bracts that appear in the centre.

---

**Flower type:** Small Decorative
**Average height:** 120–150cm (48–60in)
**Average spread:** 50cm (20in)
**Flower size:** 10–15cm (4–6in)
**Foliage:** Green
**Staking:** Preferred
**As a cut flower:** Good
**In the garden:** Excellent
**Alternative varieties:** Chat Noir, Karma Choc

# Labyrinth

When Vincent van Gogh painted his famous vases of sunflowers in honour of a visit by his painter friend Paul Gauguin, he undertook an artistic experiment – to produce an image using just three blended shades of yellow, with no loss of texture or eloquence.

Had van Gogh instead painted dahlias, he must surely have chosen Labyrinth as his subject. The shaggy, shapely fluster of petals is relaxed and romantic. The palette of colour is at the same time intriguingly complex and charmingly simple – pink-peach and apricot, darkening to raspberry ice towards the centre. The hues are blended and streaked as if a brush had pulled oil paint across the canvas.

There is beauty in all stages in a flower and these twirling petals form a compelling, evolving picture that draws you in, keeping you watching as the flowers open, bloom, mature and fade. Life imitating art in a truly inspiring way.

---

**Flower type:** Small Decorative
**Average height:** 90cm (36in)
**Average spread:** 60–75cm (24–30in)
**Flower size:** 10–15cm (4–6in)
**Foliage:** Green
**Staking:** Well-grown plants with heavy heads may benefit from staking
**As a cut flower:** A real performer
**In the garden:** Lovely border addition
**Alternative varieties:** Café au Lait, Sierra Glow

# Fascination

This eye-popping hottie combines neon-pink flowers with inky, purple-black foliage in a style statement that is anything but shy and retiring.

The blowsy, semi-double flowers bleed to a deeper hue towards the centre, where the bloom is anchored by a chocolatey central disc with a coronet of glowing stamens.

More compact than some at 60–100cm (24–40in), Fascination was bred in the UK by Elsdon in 1964 and achieved a Royal Horticultural Society Award of Garden Merit in 1994.

But age and horticultural gravitas detract not one iota from a botanical party animal that can't help but add a frisson of excitement to the garden. This lovely, lively dahlia fills up the border with impossibly funky, hot-pink daisies that pop and fizz against their black background, and entice bees and butterflies to join the show.

Try planting it with *Salvia guaranitica* 'Super Trouper' for a fresh and vivid display.

---

**Flower type:** Peony (sometimes categorized as Miscellaneous)
**Average height:** 60–100cm (24–40in)
**Average spread:** 50cm (20in)
**Flower size:** 12–15cm (5–6in)
**Foliage:** Purple-black
**Staking:** You'll probably get away without in a reasonably sheltered spot
**As a cut flower:** As good as any
**In the garden:** Its compact size means it is good for smaller gardens and containers; attractive to pollinators
**Alternative varieties:** Magenta Star is taller, while Roxy is usually shorter

# Chimborazo

Chimborazo is a volcano in Ecuador and it is bit of a dark horse. Not only is it the highest mountain in the country, but measured from the centre of the Earth rather than from sea level, it is also the highest point on the planet because it is situated on the equatorial bulge.

Which is all rather exciting to know (although it must be disappointing if you have climbed Everest). So, as one might imagine, Chimborazo-the-dahlia is a very good flower indeed, and like the volcano, has hidden depths.

Raised in the UK sometime prior to 1945, it has buds that are subtly striped with green and bronze, and the emerging flowers are at first intriguingly spidery. The petals are deep crimson-red and a yellow collar licks like flames around the disc in a fiery fashion, reminiscent of smouldering lava waiting to erupt in the garden.

As dahlias go, it has long, spare, wiry stems, which mean that the buds and flowers sit well above the foliage. All in all, Chimborazo is a stylish and elegant addition to vase or border.

---

**Flower Type:** Collerette
**Average height:** 100–150cm (40–60in)
**Average spread:** 50cm (20in)
**Flower size:** up to 14cm (5½in)
**Foliage:** Green
**Staking:** Only if grown by itself or in an exposed spot
**As a cut flower:** Fabulous and festive
**In the garden:** Looks wonderful with grasses and also with *Rudbeckia* 'Irish Eyes', whose yellow colour picks up that of the dahlia's central disc. Attractive to wildlife
**Alternative varieties:** Kaiser Walter or try Christmas Carol for planting in containers

# Fire Magic

This show-stopping American-bred dahlia was introduced in 1991 and has captivated and enthralled its public ever since. Like a nuclear sunset, it is a spectacular combination of smoky fuchsia-pink and orange, bleeding to a magenta centre. The petals are yellow-green at the base and dusted with gold, giving the flower an otherworldly metallic sheen.

Wildly floriferous, it flames and crackles magnificently in the border and is spectacular in a vase. A bold and unusual beauty, it might literally draw moths to its flame and make sunflowers want to retire, but it is sweet and gentle at heart.

Grow with single, hot-pink dahlias and with dark red flowers or foliage for a riot of colour.

---

**Flower type:** Small Semi-Cactus
**Average height:** 135cm (54in)
**Average spread:** 60cm (24in)
**Flower size:** 10–15cm (4–6in)
**Foliage:** Green
**Staking:** Yes
**As a cut flower:** Very good
**In the garden:** Stands out from the crowd and is a good back-of-the border plant
**Alternative varieties:** Waltzing Mathilda, Wannabee, Hollyhill Margarita

Series
# Karma

In the early days of dahlia growing, the surprise at discovering a plant that hybridized so gleefully was rapidly followed by some very serious people setting up exhibition categories and trying to grow the most perfect blooms possible. The poor dahlia then suffered the double ignominy of being seen as a rather rigid series of balls, followed by widespread castigation as the epitome of vulgarity.

But with a new century, dahlias have staged a comeback away from the show bench and the fashion police, and are now much beloved of florists, both professional and amateur.

The Karma Series of dahlias was bred with flower arranging in mind. They are not all of the same classification, but they are uniform in bloom and have long, strong, straight stems. They are designed to last well in water and, critically, not to require the bearer of a pretty posy to have the muscles of a weightlifter.

Karma dahlias tend to be Waterlily or Semi-Cactus types and come in a wide range of colours – the fresh whites of Karma Serena, the tequila sunset of Karma Sangria, crimson Karma Fiesta and sugar-mouse Karma Pink Corona.

# Karma Choc

One of the most popular and outstanding of the Series is the Waterlily Karma Choc – or Karma Chocolate as it is sometimes known. The inspiration must have come from the better sort of chocolate, too – the really good stuff laden with cocoa solids, that is bittersweet and melting on the tongue – because there is nothing cheap, sugary or shiny about this flower.

The sturdy plants are moderate in size and produce a mass of blooms – big enough to have impact in a border or bouquet, but small enough not to overwhelm. Each flower is held proud on dark stems above plummy-green foliage. The inky centres lighten imperceptibly to velvety dark red at the tips.

Receiving an Award of Garden Merit from the RHS in 2013, this delicious dahlia provides a rare depth of colour in the garden and looks at its best next to something bright: oranges and pinks and lime-green foliage, for example. Keep on top of the deadheading to avoid mildew.

---

**Flower type:** Small Waterlily
**Average height:** 70–80cm (28–32in)
**Average spread:** 50cm (20in)
**Flower size:** 10–15cm (4–6in)
**Foliage:** Dark green-bronze
**Staking:** You'll get away without if you grow it in a sheltered border
**As a cut flower:** Bred to excel; few, if any, are better
**In the garden:** Looks lovely near the front of the herbaceous border and will thrive when grown in large containers
**Alternative varieties:** Although they have green foliage, Lights Out, Arabian Night and the smaller-flowered La Recoleta have flowers of a comparable inky hue. Happy Single Romeo is dark red with dark foliage, but with a single flower

# CLASSIC AND ELEGANT

# Ambition

Bouncing out of the borders, Ambition is energetic both in shape and hue. A pert, purple Semi-Cactus dahlia, it is eye-poppingly bright with a funky, spiky shape that looks great in mixed company.

Plant it alongside dark foliage; with other dahlias, and combine with *Monarda* 'Cambridge Scarlet', mauve phlox, billowing *Eupatorium* and acid-yellow plants, such as goldenrod. *Ricinus communis* 'New Zealand Purple' and *Miscanthus sinensis* 'Flamingo' also make good companions.

The elongated petals and relatively small flowers make Ambition fairly resistant to wind and rain. It does not get too top-heavy in the wet so it lasts well in the garden. It also makes an excellent cut flower.

It was introduced in the Netherlands in 1961.

---

**Flower type:** Medium Semi-Cactus
**Average height:** 100–150cm (40–60in)
**Average spread:** 50cm (20in)
**Flower size:** 15–20cm (6–8in)
**Foliage:** Green
**Staking:** Not usually needed if you grow it alongside other plants
**As a cut flower:** Packs a punch!
**In the garden:** A real doer with flowers that last well
**Alternative varieties:** Purple Gem

# *Dahlia merckii*

This species dahlia is a world – or possibly 450 years of botanical interest and various forms of breeding – away from the giant Dinner-Plate dahlias that are currently so fashionable on the floristry circuit. But it has a delicate and airy charm all of its own.

It is a relatively small, spare shrub with a loose and rambling habit, which makes staking fairly irrelevant. The small flowers are a gentle lilac colour with a neat gold boss in the middle, carried on long stems and borne in profusion.

While it can look a little feeble to start with, *Dahlia merckii* will bulk up with time, but it does like plenty to drink, so don't let it dry out.

Grow it through the border where it will contribute to the orchestra, rather than being the star of the show. It looks nice with pink daisies such as *Cosmos bipinnatus* 'Sea Shells' or teamed with orange flowers and grasses.

---

**Flower type:** Species with single flowers
**Average height:** approx. 100cm (40in)
**Average spread:** 50–70cm (20–28cm)
**Flower size:** 5cm (2in)
**Foliage:** Green
**Staking:** Can be staked but looks nicer allowed to ramble through the border
**As a cut flower:** A pretty addition to a delicate, naturalistic posy
**In the garden:** Blends well with other herbaceous plants and grasses in a mixed border
**Alternative varieties:** Most of the dahlias we grow are hybrids, and although many of the newer species have been bred by crossing desirable cultivars with the species forms, being a pure species, *Dahlia merckii* is unique in character. There are not, therefore, any real alternatives but fortunately the plant is widely available.

# Spartacus

This sumptuous, red-plush dahlia is named for the classic slave-hero of legend, repeatedly made famous on the silver screen.

Spartacus was a Thracian gladiator born around 111BC. He escaped slavery to become one of the leaders of a major slave uprising against the Roman Empire and proved himself a great strategist and tactician. The contemporary documentation of his life and death is incomplete and contradictory but, in the twentieth century, Spartacus became something of a Communist and Socialist icon through his noble character and championing of the slave-underdog. He was even described by Karl Marx as 'The most splendid fellow in the whole of ancient history'.

A splendid fellow clearly deserves a splendid dahlia and there are few more splendid than Spartacus. A handsome flower on a robust plant, the colour is strong but also sophisticated. The wide petals curl slightly at the tips and are swept back like a lion's mane, and like the hero after which it is named, Spartacus can withstand a bit of bad weather, too.

Introduced in the USA in 1993, Spartacus has been a very successful performer in American dahlia shows.

---

**Flower type:** Large Decorative
**Average height:** 100cm (40in)
**Average spread:** 80cm (32in)
**Flower size:** 20–25cm (8–10in)
**Foliage:** Green
**Staking:** A good idea if the plant is well grown
**As a cut flower:** Good; cut while the blooms are still young and fresh
**In the garden:** Its strong looks make a splash
**Alternative varieties:** Black Monarch, Zorro

# White Alva's

A sport of yellow Dinner-Plate dahlia Alva's Supreme, White Alva's was introduced in the UK in 1979 and received an Award of Garden Merit from the Royal Horticultural Society in 1997.

A fantastically ornamental specimen, the flower is pure white with a hint of butter at the base of the petals, echoing its parent. The strong stems hold the blooms well above the foliage, making it a popular multi-purpose flower.

It is on the large side for cutting but it would make a fabulous centrepiece at a white wedding or grand dinner party. Create the vintage look with cream and blush-pink roses, and with smaller white dahlia flowers such as L'Ancresse combined with fresh blue-green or grey foliage like eucalyptus and dusty miller – *Centaurea cineraria* subsp. *cineraria*. Or team with variegated pineapple mint, long-stemmed sweet peas, cottage-garden blooms and airy grasses for an informal scented arrangement.

---

**Flower type:** Giant Formal Decorative
**Average height:** 130–140cm (52–56in)
**Average spread:** 50–100cm (20–40in)
**Flower size:** over 25cm (10in)
**Foliage:** Green
**Staking:** Yes, those heavy heads need it
**As a cut flower:** A dramatic centrepiece; cut very fresh and re-cut the stems under water
**In the garden:** The large flowers float above the border like a flurry of overweight snowflakes. Team with eupatorium, tall euphorbias and *Verbena bonariensis* or plant in front of dark-leaved shrubs and evergreens
**Alternative varieties:** Silver City for white, or try Alva's Supreme in yellow or Louie Meggos in cream

# Chat Noir

With sumptuously rich, garnet-red flowers deepening almost to black in the centre, and with proud and dramatic recurved petals, this established dahlia is deservedly well known and well loved.

Chat Noir means 'black cat' in French and, with its pointed florets on end, the flower could be likened to a startled feline, a ball of readiness, back arched, claws extended and fur sticking out in all directions.

And with black cats representing good luck in Britain and Japan, and prosperity in Scotland – although other countries may be more equivocal – this seems as good a reason as any to fill one's garden with this striking spiky dahlia.

Chat Noir was honoured with a Royal Horticultural Society Award of Garden Merit in 2013.

---

**Flower type:** Semi-Cactus
**Average height:** 110–150cm (44–60in)
**Average spread:** 45–80cm (18–32in)
**Flower size:** 10–15cm (4–6in)
**Foliage:** Green
**Staking:** Yes
**As a cut flower:** Bold and handsome with a good vase life
**In the garden:** Superb in the border and good in containers, too
**Alternative varieties:** Rip City, Arabian Night

# Franz Kafka

A flower with literary connotations, this tight, neat, purple dahlia is named after Franz Kafka, one of the major figures of twentieth-century literature, who was born in Prague, now in the Czech Republic, in 1883.

His work has the reputation for being rather tortured. It fuses realism and fantasy, and his protagonists often face bizarre, surreal situations redolent of absurdity and existential anxiety. As a result, 'Kafkaesque' has become a common term for things that are convoluted, absurd and frustratingly bureaucratic.

The florets of this Miniature Ball dahlia follow the Fibonacci series (see page 122), spiralling out in a pattern that might, I suppose, be considered complex or convoluted. But then again, Kafka himself was capable of statements of extraordinary insight – rising above social contortion to put his finger on the pulse of humanity.

The dahlia is charming. Free-flowering. Easy to mix in the border. Each lofty, purple punctuation point expands from dainty lime-green buds. As Kafka himself said, 'Youth is happy because it has the ability to see beauty. Anyone who keeps the ability to see beauty never grows old.' And this is a beautiful flower indeed.

---

**Flower type:** Miniature Ball (in the UK it is classed as a Large Pompon)
**Average height:** 80–100cm (32–40in)
**Average spread:** 70cm (28in)
**Flower size:** 5–10cm (2–4in)
**Foliage:** Green
**Staking:** Not usually
**As a cut flower:** Excellent
**In the garden:** Looks lovely with oranges and lime greens
**Alternative varieties:** Nijinksy is a larger purple variety, while Genova is a pretty white-and-purple blended Ball dahlia

Series
# Bishop

The Bishop Series of dahlias is one of the most well-known, recognizable and influential 'names' in the dahlia pantheon. And the grandaddy of them all, Bishop of Llandaff, played a substantial role in bringing dahlias in from the cold and dispelling the aura of disapproval that blighted their use for a hefty chunk of the twentieth century.

Bishop of Llandaff was raised by Fred Treseder of W. Treseder Ltd in the UK in the 1920s. At first classified as a Charm dahlia and later as a Peony, it is a dark crimson-red with dark foliage. It was originally named Bishop Hughes after Joshua Pritchard Hughes, whose seat was at the Cathedral Church of St Peter and St Paul in the Village of Llandaff, near Cardiff in Wales. However, it is said that the Bishop himself demurred, so the name was changed to Bishop of Llandaff.

And that was more or less that for nearly eight decades. But in the first years of the twenty-first century, hot planting schemes and tropical borders became very fashionable indeed. With brilliant flowers and smouldering foliage, Bishop of Llandaff was perfect and its popularity escalated exponentially.

So it was that, between 2002 and 2005, Dutch breeder Arnold Linden introduced a whole synod of new Bishops: Auckland, Dover, Canterbury, Lancaster, Leicester, Oxford, and York (see opposite). All of these are Peony or Single forms in various colours, although Bishops exist in other classifications, too. Each has dark foliage and they remain highly popular.

# Bishop of Dover

This Bishop is a Single rather than a Peony type, and has lovely ivory flowers with the merest veining of lilac. These are carried above the same dark, luxurious foliage as its brethren, which ranges from green-bronze and black-crimson-purple to almost black across the Series.

Try combining it with other herbaceous plants and annuals such as cosmos, agapanthus and salvias. It will also mingle well alongside soft pink shrub roses and it looks lovely in a white garden. The inky leaves do need a careful touch as they can absorb light like a black hole in the garden; but get it right and it is a strong look.

An easy-to-grow and healthy plant, Bishop of Dover is a good variety for beginners and it adds a freshness and intensity to planting schemes.

The Series has a Bishop to suit all tastes and, like other named cultivars, these are propagated and conserved by taking cuttings. But a recent development is Bishop's Children, a seed collection that produces a mixture of different heights and a range of rich colours – pink, dark red, yellow and orange. A vibrant, variable and fun twist on the theme.

---

**Flower type:** Single
**Average height:** 90–110cm (36–44in)
**Average spread:** 50cm (20in)
**Flower size:** 6cm (2½in)
**Foliage:** Dark and fabulous
**Staking:** Requires little or no support
**As a cut flower:** Good
**In the garden:** Superb in the border and good in containers, too
**Alternative varieties:** Twyning's After Eight

# Taratahi Ruby

This gorgeous little gem from New Zealand bears prolific scarlet-orange flowers and was honoured with a Royal Horticultural Society Award of Garden Merit in 2000. The tidy, regular blooms have a twist of mandarin and lime at the centre, and are carried on maroon stems.

Taratahi Ruby is a vigorous and healthy plant that adapts itself to all sorts of situations. It cuts well for floristry and acquits itself well on the show bench, too. In the garden, it looks particularly beautiful beaded with dew.

Plant in a border with other hot-coloured flowers such as orange zinnias and darker red dahlias over a smouldering carpet of nasturtiums. Or use it as a pop of colour in a cooler scheme, with soft grasses such as *Calamagrostis × acutiflora* 'Karl Foerster' and *Pennisetum villosum*, and gentle pink-green sedums. The neat flowers also look pretty with other dahlias, cut as single stems in small multi-coloured vases.

---

**Flower type:** Small Waterlily
**Average height:** 120cm (48in)
**Average spread:** 60cm (24in)
**Flower size:** 10–15cm (4–6in)
**Foliage:** Mid-green
**Staking:** Yes
**As a cut flower:** Superb
**In the garden:** Combine with other plants to soften its leggy qualities. Its robust shade of red looks great in a hot border or contrasted with dark foliage
**Alternative varieties:** Maks Royal Ruby, Karma Irene, Edwin's Sunset

# David Howard

If there were a popularity award for dahlias, then David Howard would certainly be in the running.

A stocky, sturdy and gloriously floriferous plant, the bronze-and-black buds burst into a handsome Decorative flower that is coloured somewhere between bronze and dark tangerine. The dark, coppery foliage provides a fabulous backdrop to the orange flowers and the overall effect is very striking. There are few Decorative dahlias that have dark foliage – it is far more common in Single varieties – and this is one of the features that make it an outstanding variety.

Receiving a Royal Horticultural Society Award of Garden Merit in 1995, David Howard looks great with reds, oranges, cool blues and dark purples. Team it with deep orange *Tithonia rotundifolia* 'Torch', *Helenium* 'Ruby Tuesday' and *Salvia* 'Amistad' in a hot border, use it as a chunky bedding plant or let it loose with all company in the herbaceous border.

---

**Flower type:** Miniature Decorative
**Average height:** 90–125cm (36–50in)
**Average spread:** 40cm (16in)
**Flower size:** 8–10cm (3½–4in)
**Foliage:** Dark bronze
**Staking:** Sturdy, may not require support
**As a cut flower:** A good, handsome bloom
**In the garden:** Fabulous and floriferous in the border and great in containers, too
**Alternative varieties:** David's Choice, Oakwood Naranga, Orange Keith's Choice

# Honka

Single Orchid dahlias, or Star dahlias as they are sometimes known, have flowerheads with a single ring of outer florets surrounding the central disc. These florets are uniformly either incurved (curved forwards) or recurved (bending backwards).

One might be forgiven for looking twice at Honka before recognizing it as part of the dahlia family. The flowers are pared-back, minimalist even. Reduced to about eight narrow, creamy yellow petals, they are carried in profusion over the small bush like so many delicate stars.

But is it a pretty, dainty little thing and well worth having in the garden. Dahlias are rarely scented but when they are, it is usually the Single Orchid varieties that smell sweet, and the Honka Series have a gentle perfume if you get close enough. The plants are compact and the flowers carried on sturdy stems, so they are perfect for planting in tubs or as part of a golden summer border alongside achilleas, the smaller burnets (*Sanguisorba* species) and verbascums, or with baptisias and salvias.

---

**Flower type:** Single Orchid (sometimes known as Star dahlias)
**Average height:** 60–100cm (24–40in)
**Average spread:** 40–50cm (16–20in)
**Flower size:** 10–12cm (4–5in)
**Foliage:** Green
**Staking:** Short enough that it probably won't need staking unless it is very well fed
**As a cut flower:** Makes a very happy arrangement
**In the garden:** Good performer
**Alternative varieties:** There are several Honka varieties, including Honka Red and Honka Surprise, which is deep pink and yellow, while Juul's Allstar is another Orchid dahlia, which looks like a pretty pink-and-yellow pinwheel

# Doris Day

One of the highest-flying stars of stage and screen during the twentieth century was Doris Day. Singer and actress, she was possessed of a glorious smile and wholesome media persona which, coupled with a fearsome drive and focus, and a steely resolve, saw her enjoy a career that spanned six decades.

She starred in many films that were to become classics, including *Calamity Jane*, *Pillow Talk* and *Love Me or Leave Me*, and her musical partners included Frank Sinatra. The eponymous dahlia was named by C. S. Weijers and Sons in Holland in 1952, a decade when Doris Day was arguably at the height of her fame.

It is a dahlia that befits a star – pert, pretty and generous – and is a trooper in the garden as well. It is a compact bush and, kept well-fed and deadheaded, it will produce cardinal-red flowers almost continually throughout the summer. It has had some success on the show bench but it is in the garden, splashing colour around with style and glamour, that the bold, red-carpet quality shines through.

Doris Day received a Royal Horticultural Society Award of Garden Merit in 1960.

---

**Flower Type:** Small Cactus
**Average height:** 90–125cm (36–50in)
**Average spread:** 45cm (18in)
**Flower size:** 10–15cm (4–6in)
**Foliage:** Green
**Staking:** No
**As a cut flower:** Very good
**In the garden:** Lovely compact bush
**Alternative varieties:** Kenora Sunset

# Buttercup

Raised in Australia in 1971, Buttercup is a little ball of antipodean sunshine, as cheerful and laid-back as they come. From a distance, it does indeed bear some passing resemblance to a highly bred double ranunculus, or perhaps santolina on steroids – round, yellow drumstick flowers with a hint of darker orange where the petals are yet to fully unfurl. The flowers are prolifically produced and held up above the foliage on purple stems.

Pompon dahlias are very similar to Ball dahlias, with the same tightly packed pattern of florets. But Pompons are smaller and more spherical, so they are arguably less dramatic and more good-natured about fitting into the garden. They don't steal the show in a bouquet, either.

---

**Flower type:** Pompon
**Average height:** 70–90cm (28–36in)
**Average spread:** 80cm (32in)
**Flower size:** up to 5cm (2in)
**Foliage:** Green
**Staking:** No
**As a cut flower:** Good
**In the garden:** A useful plant, the tight balls can be used to add focus and punctuation to a scheme of airy foliage and small flowers
**Alternative varieties:** Golden Sceptre, Sunny Boy

# Twyning's After Eight

Sometimes it is the simplest flowers that have the biggest 'wow' factor. And for elegance, minimalism and impact, you have to go a long way to beat Twyning's After Eight.

This is one of a number of delightful dahlias bred by Mark Twyning of the National Dahlia Collection in Cornwall. Mark has an eagle eye for small differences that might make a promising new cultivar – whether it is picking outstanding seedlings from open-pollinated plants or taking cuttings from an established variety that has sported (developed morphological differences from the rest of the plant). A significant number of his plants, such as Twyning's Revel and Twyning's Smartie, are named after sweets. Twyning's After Eight is no different, recalling the famous after-dinner mint with a white, mint fondant centre and dark chocolate coating.

The plant forms attractive mounds of chocolate-black foliage, and the more sun it gets, the blacker it becomes. The small flowers are classy, too: pure white but for the softest of pink flushes along the veins and a warm yellow central disc. The contrast is dramatic and appealing. The flowers are relatively small – so usefully, they don't struggle with rain.

Robust and weather-resistant, this is an incredibly popular plant. In the garden its foliage is a good foil for other plants and it is a very good container specimen, too. Twyning's After Eight received a Royal Horticultural Society Award of Garden Merit in 2004.

---

**Flower type:** Single
**Average height:** 90–120cm (36–48in)
**Average spread:** 45–60cm (18–24in)
**Flower size:** 8cm (3½in)
**Foliage:** Dark chocolate
**Staking:** No
**As a cut flower:** Wonderful
**In the garden:** A beautiful and striking plant, attractive to gardeners and to pollinators. Perfect in a white garden as the sultry, dark foliage will add impact and weight to foliage that is otherwise predominantly green or silver
**Alternative varieties:** Joe Swift is similar but has a darker centre

# Cornel

Since its introduction by Dutch dahlia breeder Cor Geerlings in 1994, Cornel has proven itself a consistent performer.

Classified as a Small Ball dahlia, the intense colour and crisply defined shape have great border impact, drawing the eye and bouncing it from one bloom to the next. The bronzy buds expand into neat, perfectly formed globes of rich maroon and the petals reflex evenly back to the stem.

Its strong, straight stems have endeared it to gardeners over the years and it also excels as a cut flower. The warm, slightly earthy red looks particularly good in autumn wedding bouquets and other arrangements, accompanied by gold and bronze flowers and leaves.

---

**Flower type:** Small Ball
**Average height:** 120cm (48in)
**Average spread:** 40cm (16in)
**Flower size:** 10–15cm (4–6in)
**Foliage:** Green
**Staking:** Benefits from staking
**As a cut flower:** Outstanding
**In the garden:** Equally good in the border and in containers
**Alternative varieties:** Prom, Natal

# Clair de Lune

This exquisite, moon-touched flower is almost too perfect to be real. The deep buttercup central disc is surrounded by a fluffy collar of lemon-sorbet petals that, in turn, sit within a halo of pearly, gold-dust-sprinkled, lemon ray florets. Subtle and dreamy, it is a symphony in yellow.

In the garden, it adds a clear brightness and brings out the colour in plants such as variegated miscanthus and lime-green alchemilla, while also working well with the small daisy-like flowers of feverfew and delicate *Ammi majus* and gypsophila.

Introduced in 1946, Clair de Lune received a Royal Horticultural Society Award of Garden Merit in 1995 and is a regular on the UK show circuit.

---

**Flower type:** Collerette
**Average height:** 100–150cm (40–60in)
**Average spread:** 50cm (20in)
**Flower size:** 5–10cm (2–4in)
**Foliage:** Green
**Staking:** Not usually necessary in the border
**As a cut flower:** Excellent
**In the garden:** Produces abundant blooms and the bees love it
**Alternative varieties:** Yellow Bird, Impression Fortuna or, for a yellow Collerette with a hint of pink, try Apple Blossom

# Kenora Challenger

This beautiful ivory Semi-Cactus dahlia is poignantly named in honour of the *Challenger* space shuttle that broke up shortly after take-off in 1986 with the loss of all crew. The flight was particularly high-profile thanks to the presence of Christa McAuliffe, who was to have been the first teacher and ordinary American citizen in space. This brought the tragedy particularly close to home for American dahlia breeder Gordon Leroux, whose wife was also a teacher.

The flowers of Kenora Challenger form dense stars, with the petals sharp at the tips but broader and less tightly furled at the base. Their size and colour make them a very high-impact border flower and they look fantastic as part of a white garden, especially at dusk. It is also a first-class variety for showing.

---

**Flower type:** Large Semi-Cactus
**Average height:** 120cm (48in)
**Average spread:** 30cm (12in)
**Flower size:** 20–25cm (8–10in)
**Foliage:** Green
**Staking:** Advised
**As a cut flower:** Good
**In the garden:** Lovely bold shape in the border; looks particularly good at dusk
**Alternative varieties:** White Star, the Fimbriated Cactus Haseley Bridal Wish or, for a frilly, fimbriated snowstorm of a dahlia, try Tsuki-yori-no-shisha

# GROWING AND CARE

GIVEN THE RIGHT CONDITIONS, DAHLIAS ARE EASY TO GROW – THE TRICK IS KNOWING WHAT THOSE CONDITIONS ARE AND THEN CHOOSING THE PLANTS THAT SUIT YOU BEST. THERE ARE TRIALS AND TRIBULATIONS IN ALL GARDENING ENDEAVOURS; THE VERY BEST GARDENERS HAVE PLANTS THAT GET NIBBLED BY PESTS OR SNAPPED BY FROST. WHAT IS IMPORTANT IS LEARNING AS YOU GO, AND ENJOYING THE PROCESS EVERY STEP OF THE WAY.

## Cultivation

Despite possessing extensive charms, dahlias do have their detractors. Grown for exhibition for generations, the association with painstaking cultivation, immaculate blooms and enormous flowers that don't require staking as much as scaffolding, dies hard.

Also, the prospect that one's cherished tubers may come to nothing more than expensive slug food is of real concern. I know this only too well. The first time I tried to grow dahlias, the summer was wet and the lush competing growth cast too much shade. I was distracted for a couple of critical weeks and returned to find pots of slimy stumps in urgent need of rescue. The story has a happy ending, however. A little bit of TLC and a lot of food and water later, those very tubers are thriving happily in my garden, now big and robust enough to laugh in the face of adversity.

Given the right conditions, dahlias are actually easy and enjoyable to grow – and this is the nub of the matter. There is really only one rule to gardening: give a plant what it needs and it will reward you handsomely. Guard your dahlias fiercely against frost, make sure they get plenty of sun and nourishment, and the tubers will perform. There are few plants that grow so big so fast, and flower so consistently and splendiferously all summer.

So take a good look at how much space you have, identify your most dahlia-friendly spot, and experiment with a few that take your fancy.

## Selecting varieties

Regardless of size and classification, dahlias all like warmth, light and rich living. Everything else is about you – where you want to put them, your personal tastes in colour and form, and what function you want them to perform. Then simply leaf through a catalogue and pick varieties that fit your space and available time.

As already explored, dahlias come in many shapes and sizes. Big plants that look fantastic in a large border, potager or cutting garden may swamp an urban courtyard or be less suitable for containers. In a domestic garden, it is usually desirable to incorporate dahlias amid existing planting, in which case visiting other gardens to familiarize yourself with a few different varieties and good design combinations can pay dividends.

When first dipping an experimental toe in the water, it is a good idea to choose plants that are known for being healthy and robust, such as David Howard, Happy Single Flame or Moonfire. Dwarf dahlias and those that form a modest bush won't get out of hand, and these smaller plants will be more manageable in their demands for staking, food and water. Learn how dahlias tick first, then, when you are thoroughly addicted and you pack your plot with dazzling and extravagant colour, success will be second nature and plants will thrive.

Finally, pick the plants that you really like best. Single dahlias with dark foliage are fashionable, as are the dark reds and dramatic Dinner-Plates, but if your taste is for Bicolour Fimbriated Cactus dahlias that look as if they've got lost on the way to a drag-queen convention, then go for it, and be proud to do so.

## Buying dahlias

Depending on the time of year you are shopping for them, dahlias are available as tubers, as rooted cuttings or in pots.

Dahlia tubers are made up of a handful of roots, plump tentacles dangling from a central hub, or crown, which is the base of last year's stem. The fleshy roots store food to get the plant started in spring, a bit like a seed potato does, and the crown comprises a cluster of growing shoots called 'eyes'.

When you are buying dahlias, it is important to pick specimens that are as healthy as possible. The tubers should be firm, rather than dry or shrivelled, and there should be no sign of rot, mould or damage. Avoid tubers that have broken into pieces – for the plant to grow you need at least one eye attached to the piece of root, and preferably several.

Tubers and rooted cuttings are the most cost-effective way to buy dahlias. Start browsing catalogues and supplier websites in autumn and aim to order them before midwinter. By early spring, tubers will also be available to buy in nurseries and garden centres.

Suppliers will send out tubers and cuttings in mid-spring at the point where they can be started into growth. Pot up the cuttings in gritty compost as soon as possible after they arrive and put them somewhere warm. Remember that dahlias are not hardy, so the tubers need to be protected from frost, both when they are dormant and after they have started to grow.

Later in the year, you will also be able to buy plants in growth and flower from garden retailers. The great advantage to these is that you can see you are getting the plant you want (mislabelling is fairly rare, but it can happen). You can also check the leaves for any spotting or mottling that could be a sign of disease. The disadvantage is that you will pay very much more for the plant than if you bought it as a tuber or cutting. But if you just want a few to see how you get on, then tubs of dahlias, potted up and ready to go, are a great place to start.

## Climate

Dahlias are native to Mexico and having evolved in a sub-tropical climate, they are tender, or half hardy at best. In colder areas, they cannot be left outdoors in winter.

In terms of climate zones, they are generally safe in USDA Zone 8 and above, and classify, very roughly, as RHS H3 and European Hardiness Zone 9. As a rule of thumb, no matter where in the world you are, the more warm, moist and sunny the climate, the happier your dahlias will be. In marginal areas, as long as the soil is well drained and not too heavy, it is possible to overwinter the tubers in the ground with the application of a thick blanket of mulch.

You can cultivate dahlias even in places where the weather is more extreme, as long as you are prepared to extend the growing season by keeping them artificially warm and bright, taking advantage of microclimates, or, in drier areas, making sure that they are watered liberally. The trick is to become familiar with your conditions and experiment with the plants – winters vary and your dahlias may surprise you.

## Situation and soil

Dahlias like lots of light and are best planted in full sun, although they will take a little shade if they must. The warmer the spot, the better they will thrive, and a sheltered position also helps to reduce weather damage – particularly important with the larger blooms and taller plants.

While dahlias are fairly tolerant when it comes to soil, a bit of preparation goes a long way. Although they like plenty of moisture, they can't bear being waterlogged, and if planted in cold, heavy soil, they may struggle to get started in spring. At the other end of the spectrum, they will be hungry on thin, poor ground that is prone to drought.

Therefore, whether your soil is heavy or light to start with, aim for that horticultural holy trinity: moist, rich and free-draining. Digging in well-rotted manure or other organic matter can lighten heavy soils, which will help with overwintering in situ, as well. It will also improve the water- and nutrient-retention of sandy or chalky soils, which can then be boosted further by adding a mulch.

Professional growers often advise that dahlias be given a dedicated bed, or an area of the border that is all their own, as they don't always cope well with competition from other plants. But in an ordinary small garden like mine, this is impractical, so one must tread the line between giving the dahlias the best care that is possible, in both borders and containers, and growing other plants too.

## Planting and care

Dahlia tubers can be planted outside after frost or they can be started off in pots under glass – in a greenhouse or on a sunny windowsill – in late winter to early spring. Plant them 10–12cm (4–5in) deep with the crown uppermost. If planting directly, allow enough space between each tuber for the plants to grow to their full size without being overcrowded. Keep them moist but not wet, or the tuber may rot.

By mid-spring, you should see shoots appearing above the soil. At this point it is important to be vigilant, especially if your tubers are in the ground. Slugs love a tasty new dahlia shoot more than anything else in the world, and in a bad year they can graze the plant so hard that it does not emerge at all. If slugs are a particular problem in your garden, start your plants off in containers, which can be more easily defended.

Fend off dastardly molluscs by any means you choose; create a barrier or moat, surround them with gravel or eggshells, lift pots onto a table, go out with a torch and collect them at night, or in extremis, scatter the odd slug pellet. But the healthier and better-fed your plant is, the quicker it will grow away from the ravages of pests, so keep it in tip-top condition and it will prevail.

When the soil is warm and the risk of frost is past, harden off your pot-grown dahlias by moving them outside during the day. Put them somewhere sheltered and not too sunny, or they may scorch, and move them back inside in the evening. Keep this up for at least a week.

Plant out both pot-grown plants and tubers in late spring after enriching the soil with organic material. A little sprinkle of balanced fertilizer or pelleted chicken manure at this point is a good idea as the additional nitrogen will allow the leafy growth to bulk up quickly.

Weather is a capricious thing, so even now, watch out for late frost. If a surprise drop in temperature is forecast, move containers of dahlias back under cover or insulate plants with a layer of horticultural fleece or even an old blanket, and you'll probably get away with it.

## Containers

If you have only a small garden, or even just a courtyard or balcony, you can still grow dahlias. The newer varieties, such as the Gallery and Mystic Series, have been bred to slot neatly into smaller outside spaces and many other varieties will thrive if they are grown in a decent-sized pot.

Obviously, the bigger the container you have, the bigger the dahlia you can grow. But I confess I don't see the point of pushing this to its ultimate limits. After all, with so many lovely little creatures at our disposal, why would we struggle with those resource-intensive giants?

Plant your dahlias into pots as usual and transfer to their final container when they are big enough. Then just harden them off and move outside when the weather is warm, remembering to feed and water them well.

An additional advantage to keeping a few tubers in pots is that as summer progresses and other plants go over, you can pop a lovely bushy dahlia into any gap that appears in the border to keep it looking good.

## Feeding

Dahlias are thirsty and hungry creatures and will respond well to rich feeding and plenty of water, producing bigger and more floriferous plants. Initially, they need nitrogen to develop plenty of leafy growth and reach a good size, so until about the longest day, give them a high-nitrogen liquid feed every week after planting out. After this, continue the feeding regimen until mid-autumn, but swap to a high-potassium fertilizer to promote the production of flowers. Comfrey tea (see opposite) is high in potash and proprietary tomato fertilizer is also ideal.

Feeding is particularly important for pot-grown plants as they will quickly use up the available nutrients in the compost. If you are growing dahlias for cutting, you will particularly want to make sure that they are as well nourished as possible, as this will speed up the production of new flowers after each picking.

## Staking

The compact new dahlia cultivars have been bred to avoid the necessity of staking and, even with bigger ones, you'll probably get away with it (up to a point) if you grow them among decently supportive companions. But the taller varieties and plants grown on a more exposed site will most certainly need support.

How you go about this will be dictated by your reasons for growing the flowers and how big they are, and there will always be a slight tension between beauty and functionality.

If you are growing for showing, then a stout stake – or three – is the perfect solution; you can tie the plant in and it doesn't have to look

## COMFREY TEA AND NETTLE TEA

You can make your own organic plant food quite easily using comfrey, which can be grown specifically for the purpose, and nettles which are generally pretty easy to find. Any comfrey will do but Russian 'Bocking 14' is often recommended as it is high-yielding and less invasive than other varieties – even so, choose your site carefully as comfrey is a vigorous and long-lived plant.

Comfrey will produce a feed that is rich in potassium, which will stimulate flowers. Nettle tea is rich in nitrogen that will stimulate leafy growth. The recipe for both is identically imprecise.

Wearing gloves, acquire the plant material – it is easiest to cut whole stems just above soil level. Put approx. 1kg (2lb 4oz) of greenery into a bucket or barrel of water – 15l (3 gallons) is a good amount – and cover it. In four to six weeks you will have a stinky brown liquid – use this to water your plants once a week.

See www.gardenorganic.org.uk for more details.

pretty in the garden, just perfect on the show bench. On a domestic scale, a bamboo cane for each plant, or a teepee of twigs or brushwood that the dahlias can grow through and be tied into, and that will eventually be hidden by the foliage, will do the job nicely.

Growing dahlias as cut flowers is a kind of halfway house, and both stakes and teepees are fine. Alternatively, you can support a whole bed by putting a stout stake in each corner and a few more dotted through the planting, then weaving a cat's cradle of twine between them, pulled tight to create a supportive mesh.

Whichever support you choose, put it in at the same time as you plant your dahlias into their final positions. This avoids damaging the tubers and it will be a much easier job than wrestling with armfuls of sappy growth later on.

# Pinching out

When the plants have three to four true pairs of leaves, pinch out the growing tips to encourage

the formation of bushy plants, and help avoid the stems becoming leggy.

Pinching will result in more side shoots and these will produce more flowers. For a large number of smaller flowers – for floristry, for example – just let them grow, but if you want fewer, larger flowers, nip off a few buds per stem and the plant will direct its energy to those that remain.

## Deadheading and ongoing maintenance

Once the dahlias have been planted outside and there really is no risk of frost, they are fairly low-maintenance. As discussed, keep them well fed and watered – paying particular attention to watering in dry weather – and the first flowers will appear around midsummer, depending on when the tubers were planted.

Deadhead regularly to ensure that the plant keeps producing new buds. Picking does the same job and the more you pick the more flowers you get. And, all being well, your plants should bloom until the first frosts.

## Propagation

We all have favourite plants we can't get enough of and laying your hands on multiple specimens of every dahlia you want can seem costly. However, a savvy gardener will soon realize that a bit of crafty propagation will rapidly fill the garden with choice varieties at a fraction of the cost of buying in new tubers or established plants.

There are several ways you can go about it: taking cuttings, dividing tubers and growing from seed to create new forms are all reasonably easy, as long as you have the space and warmth to do so. Just remember how the plant ticks, pander to its likes and dislikes, and act accordingly.

# Growing for shows

In the nineteenth and twentieth centuries, exhibition was the *raison d'être* of dahlias for many people. They are still an important part of local and national flower shows, while regional societies often hold ferocious competitions.

Growing for exhibition can be addictive and you have to give your plants the very best care you can. Forget the relaxed domestic regimen, the pursuit of perfection requires dedication. While there is also sociable fun to be had, never forget that this is a competition and your opponents will give no quarter!

Even by the standards of dahlias in general, show dahlias need lots of food and water to reach their full potential and produce the largest blooms borne on the longest, straightest stems. You will need to stake each plant thoroughly so that it is held entirely upright, and tie it in as if in pursuit of a gold medal for bondage.

### Tricks of the trade

There are various things you can do to make sure that your flowers are as fabulous as possible and that you are poised for success.

Firstly, make sure you are growing the right thing. There are local and national standards for exhibition so, before you plant, find out what the classes will be and which varieties are acceptable.

Do your homework and learn your trade.

Read and follow the show schedule and the rules. They may seem arbitrary in places, but they are The Rules and since the judges will adhere to them, to the letter, so should you.

## Growing for success

Back in the garden, plant Pompon varieties early. With this form, the second flush of flowers is often better than the first, so remove the first flowers. The idea is to create a perfect ball, with petals reflexed back to the stem; you can give nature a hand by pinching off the green calyx behind the bloom with sharp fingernails.

Show dahlias are usually grown by disbudding selected side shoots to encourage super-blooms. The number of blooms per plant should be limited to three for giant dahlias, four on large ones and six on mediums – this will ensure that the remaining flowers are as big as possible.

Disbudding sounds a little bit brutal, throwing all those would-be flowers away, but there is no room for sentimentality.

And where earwigs may be of little concern in the garden, a showman's trick is to smear a band of petroleum jelly around the flower stems, to stop the pincered pests ascending.

The bigger the flower, the more weather-sensitive it is, so a cover may be necessary. This is usually a plastic tent in a wet climate or muslin shelter if the sun is very strong.

On the day, pick your very best flowers, early in the morning and with the longest stems possible. Secure them carefully in transit so they don't thrash around and get damaged and, it goes without saying, keep them in water at all times.

## Titivating on the show bench

My first job in gardening was organizing events and garden shows. Even as a keen gardener, the level of preparation in the marquee was eye-opening. I watched vegetable exhibitors trim the tattered edges of cabbages to tidy perfection and practically scream if anyone went to touch the prized exhibit, in case they disturb the waxy bloom. 'Once your veg are ready, don't leave them even for a moment. There may be tamperers!' one hoary gentleman told me, in hushed and ominous tones.

People take it very seriously and getting your dahlias catwalk-ready is a key part of the process.

Experienced showmen will stop at nothing to make their flowers look as good as possible. Use a sharp knife or tweezers to remove any damaged petals, then use a cotton bud or small, soft paintbrush to push the adjacent petals together to hide the gap.

It is not cheating: it is improving your chances of winning – a subtle but important difference. After all, this is less gardening than it is fashion modelling and judges mark perfection they can see, not the flaws or imperfections that you have removed.

Finally, you may not win first time, but if you grow the best flowers you can with the best care you can muster, and follow the rules to the letter, you will learn a huge amount. And this will stand you in good stead the next time.

## Taking cuttings

To propagate in this fashion, buy tubers (or take your existing tubers out of storage) in early spring and plant shallowly in a pot of free-draining compost. Ideally you should put them on a heated bench or in a propagator, but a consistently warm location such as a kitchen windowsill will do. Take care not to overwater or the tubers will rot.

In a few weeks, shoots will appear around the central stem of the old tuber. Allow them to grow on in a warm, bright place. When they reach about 7cm (3in), use a sharp knife to slice them away from the base of the stem, below the lowest set of leaves. You can take up to three cuttings per tuber, but more than that risks weakening the parent.

Cut off the lower leaves and pinch out the growing tip before potting into a gritty, free-draining compost mix. Water well, cover with a polythene bag and place in a warm, bright place, out of direct sunlight. You can remove the bag after a few weeks when the cutting has taken. Keep the compost moist but not soggy and grow on somewhere bright and frost-free.

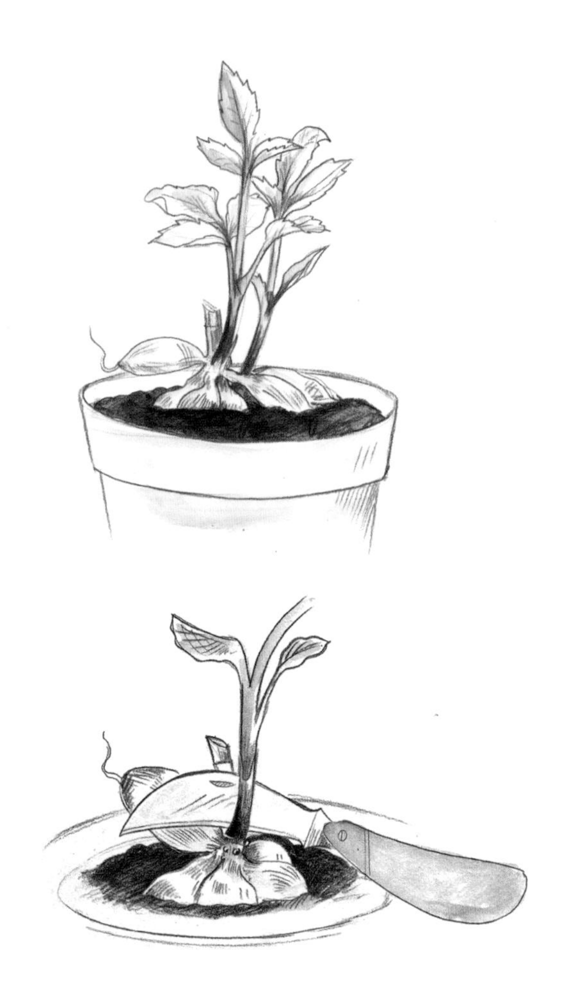

## Dividing tubers

If you don't want to take cuttings or you don't have the space, wait until mid- to late spring when your overwintered tubers are ready to grow or new ones arrive. Pick robust specimens and remove any rot or shrivelled parts with a sharp knife. If you look carefully at the crown, you should be able to see tiny shoots or eyes (see opposite), a bit like those on a potato. These start off quite small and flat, then get larger and larger as spring approaches. Use the knife to carefully cut up the tubers so each cut piece includes an eye. You should be able to make several new plants from each tuber, but

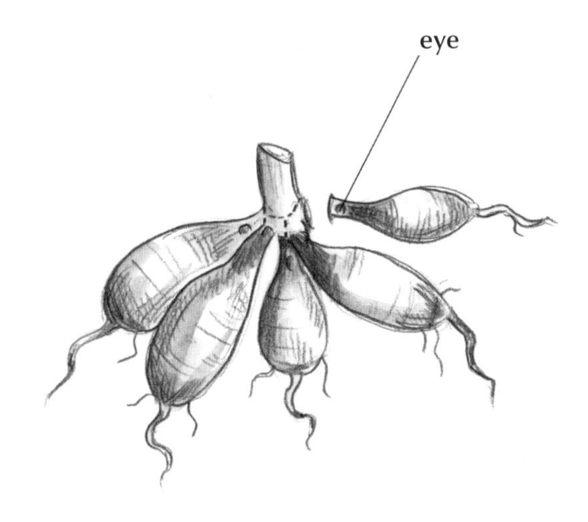


keep the cut pieces nice and chunky.

Pot each piece of dahlia tuber into gritty, free-draining compost. Keep in a bright, frost-free place. The cuttings will soon start to produce shoots. As they grow, feed and pot on until they are ready to be planted outside.

### Growing from seed

Because dahlias interbreed promiscuously, saving seed from open-pollinated plants can create all sorts of exciting and unique varieties. Professional breeders often choose promising forms from open-pollinated plants or set up deliberate crosses. The first time I visited the National Dahlia Collection near Penzance in Cornwall, there was a huge and magnificent bed of Single dahlia flowers, all of which had been grown from seed; the variations in leaf form and colour, and the differences between the flowers, were remarkable. While dahlias are marvellous, they tend to be presented as *fait accompli* cultivars but there is nothing quite like seeing a bed of inspiring flowers for the future and cultivars in the making.

It is easy to save seed from dahlias – just don't deadhead the variety you are interested in breeding from but instead let the seed pods ripen on the plant. You may shorten the flowering period a little but that is a small price to pay for the advancement of science and horticulture, as your garden knows it.

When the pods are ripe, pick them and leave them to become fully dry. Then pull each one gently apart, catching all the plant material in a container – an old plastic takeaway box is ideal. Separate the seed from the chaff (all the other leftover bits) by blowing on it gently.

Store the seed in a paper bag or envelope in a cool, dry place. In spring, sow it in compost-filled trays, cover with a further light sprinkle of compost, then place in a propagator or polythene bag on a light windowsill until seedlings emerge.

Shade the seedlings from bright sunshine and pot them up when they are about 7cm (3in) high, before hardening off and planting them out.

## Overwintering

Since dahlias are not frost-hardy (see page 216), the usual advice is to lift and store tubers over winter unless they are grown on a very sheltered and well-drained site. The process is fairly straightforward. When the first frost has blackened the foliage, use a fork to lift each plant and brush the soil off the roots – a soft household brush or medium-sized paintbrush is useful for this. Cut back the stems, turn the tubers upside down so that any residual moisture doesn't pool in the crown, and leave them to dry naturally, remembering that even now they can be damaged by cold. When they are dry, store them. Methods include wrapping them individually in newspaper or packing them in sand, compost, vermiculite or even an old blanket – it needs to be a breathable layer.

The important thing is that they remain cool, dry, dark and frost-free until spring.

But, as lifting dahlias is often seen as a chore, overwintering in the ground is not uncommon. In warmer areas, in a sheltered garden or in town, it pays to experiment. Since cold and damp are both sworn enemies of the dormant dahlia, you will have best success if your soil is gritty and free-draining, or your pots well-insulated. A really good mulch of well-rotted manure, garden compost, straw or bracken will help to insulate the tubers from a light frost. Keep your fingers crossed, offer up your prayers and, come spring, they may surprise you.

# Pests and diseases

It is better by far to grow vigorous and healthy plants than it is to recover infected and infested ones, but keeping an eye out for the most common problems means that you can respond quickly and effectively should they appear.

Faced with slugs, earwigs, aphids and mildew, the way you choose to respond is up to you. People are increasingly resorting to organic methods and while there is a range of 'chemical' options, they are better used in the case of emergency than on an ongoing basis.

My own preference is to try to garden in such a way that the pests are balanced out by the predators that rely on them, and to keep my plants healthy enough to be ahead of the game. You show me a garden, even the finest in the land, and I'll show you slug damage.

## PESTS

All gardens have pests to a greater or lesser degree; they quite literally come with the territory. But while bugs and beasts may nibble on your plants, they are also part of the ecosystem. I tend to accept that it is a battle of wills and while there will undoubtedly be a certain amount of collateral damage, a garden is more than the sum of its parts and a hint of imperfection is worth it for the pleasure of seeing butterflies, bees, and the birds that also feed on the garden undesirables.

## APHIDS

Greenfly and blackfly are a real problem and can colonize plants extremely quickly. This is bad news as, in addition to looking unsightly, their sap-sucking antics can weaken plants, distort growth and spread viruses, while large colonies attract ants that want to farm them for honeydew.

You can help the situation by keeping your garden as ecologically balanced as possible; if there are plenty of ladybirds and insect-eating birds, they will devour aphids with joy in their hearts. But there are times when a more hands-on approach is required. You can use a jet of water to blast the colonies off the plant, or there is a wide range of organic insecticide sprays based on natural compounds that are toxic to aphids. But although you may be targeting aphids, remember that the sprays may be harmful to other insects, too, including beneficial ones, so read the label carefully. The same is true for chemical and systemic insecticide sprays – if you poison the plant, you poison the things that feed on the plant, whether they are aphids or bees.

## CATERPILLARS

Dahlias are a tasty treat for various butterfly and moth larvae, but since most of us love having the adults in the garden, open warfare should be avoided.

The best thing is to be vigilant. Watch out for signs of caterpillars, such as droppings and nibbled leaves, then pick them off and rehome them. I salve my conscience by trying to identify the caterpillar and then putting it on a plant that is an acceptable alternative, as some can be quite specific about what they will eat.

## EARWIGS

Other than entomologists, I have never met anyone who really likes earwigs. That said, few regard them with the same wrath as do professional dahlia growers.

Omnivorous earwigs are primarily nocturnal and, in addition to helpfully eating insect pests, they make holes in the leaves and flowers of dahlias and clematis, in severe cases shredding them entirely. They love to hide in dark, damp places, which include the tubular ray florets of dahlia flowers, emerging when disturbed by cutting and titivating.

Part of the problem is that they are hard to dissuade (although if you are not growing for exhibition this may not trouble you overly). They are not particularly susceptible to organic controls and most gardeners will suggest creating a hidey-hole for them, in the form of a straw-stuffed flower pot upended on a cane into which the earwigs will crawl and where they can then be found and dealt with. In extreme cases, there are sprays available, but read the label carefully and be aware that these will affect other wildlife in the garden.

One solution is to reduce the number of places earwigs can lurk. Single dahlias and the more open flower forms are less susceptible to earwig damage. Try not to grow your plants next to fences or decking, for example, as these might offer daytime hiding places.

## RED SPIDER MITE

This pest is particularly insidious as you often don't notice that it is present until the colonies are well established and hard to shift. The mites themselves are minute brown arthropods that are visible to the naked eye, but only just. They form large colonies on plants in hot, dry conditions and the first you may know of them is when your plants become mottled and sickly, and you notice fine webs across the undersides of the leaves.

Because the infestation can spread rapidly, you should remove any badly affected leaves and dispose of them (preferably by burning). The mites are very small and struggle to move in damp conditions, so spraying the leaves with water can help. And because good husbandry really is the best prevention, regular application of a foliar feed such as comfrey tea (see page 219) will kill two birds with one stone.

When it comes to insecticides, proprietary sprays are available, but the same environmental reservations apply to mites as they do to aphids, so I prefer not to use them.

## SLUGS AND SNAILS

Molluscs are a menace. They love a tasty dahlia and will happily munch the leaves and flowers as well as graze the emerging shoots to oblivion if they can.

Stop at nothing to save your plants, especially early in the season. Putting them on a table outside can help, as can creating a barrier.

Stand your pot on a brick in a saucer of water, or deploy something dry or uncomfortable to crawl over, such as eggshells, or just something plain nasty, such as coffee grounds.

Creating diversions like beer traps can help, as can reducing the populations by going out with a torch at night, picking off the slimy little beasts by hand, then taking them for a long walk (ducks are always pleased to see them!) Remember to look under pots for slugs and on the dark side of pots for snails. An empty pot can provide a hidey-hole for them; they will think they are safe, but you can deal with them at your leisure.

If the worst comes to the worst, there is an increasingly good range of organic slug pellets made from ferric phosphate, and you can also treat slugs with beneficial nematodes as a biological control, which can be watered into the compost and around growing plants in spring.

Ultimately, you will probably get best results from using several different methods to keep your dahlias safe.

### VINE WEEVIL

If you plant your dahlias in the soil, vine weevils may not be much of a problem, but if you grow a lot of plants in pots, then it is only a matter of time before this particular menace raises its pointy snout.

The adults are relatively unassuming, grey-black beetles, whose tendency to amble around nibbling things is dwarfed by the havoc wreaked by the larvae, whose work under the surface of the earth goes unnoticed until it is almost too late.

The creamy C-shaped grubs have rust-coloured heads and are about 1cm (½in) long. They have a massive appetite for the roots of plants such as strawberries and heucheras, and are more than happy to add dahlias to the menu. Plants that were growing vigorously suddenly stop in their tracks and look sick. Investigation into the pot usually reveals an almost total absence of roots and the unwelcome presence of vine-weevil larvae.

Other than throwing away the compost, chucking the little menaces into the nearest fish pond, inspecting the remains of your plant carefully for stragglers, then hopefully repotting with the promise of tender loving care, the best thing to do is to control them organically using nematodes. Order these online and water into the compost when temperatures increase in spring, and in autumn when plants are still in growth.

## DISEASES

The less happy a plant is, the more likely it is to suffer from disease. Keeping plants well fed and well ventilated will undoubtedly help, but it pays to become familiar with the symptoms of viral and bacterial infections, and to act swiftly to prevent their spread if they appear.

### POWDERY MILDEWS AND FUNGAL INFECTIONS

There are various common fungal infections of dahlias and these can emerge in warm, damp and still conditions. They are a particular issue in a wet summer and in autumn, when the nights become cooler and damper.

Leaf spot is exactly what one might imagine – a light green spot on the leaf, which increases in size before going brown as the tissue dies. Powdery mildew is easily identified, too, as the leaves become covered in a dusting of greyish white powder, which, perversely, can be exacerbated by inadequate watering.

If you garden organically, the trick is, as always, to make sure that your plants are growing strongly with plenty of water at the roots, and that they are positioned in full sun. They also need good ventilation, so don't plant them too densely.

If fungus or mildew strikes, remove the worst-affected leaves, usually the lowest ones, and burn or dispose of them in the waste bin, not the compost heap.

Spraying or dusting with proprietary fungicides can help, and covering the whole plant with a spray made of skimmed cow's milk, diluted 3:7 with water, is said to have a prophylactic effect in wet summers!

## VIRUSES

It can be hard to identify viruses for certain, but if an otherwise well-kept plant presents with mottling to the leaves, distorted foliage and stunted growth, a virus is the most likely culprit. That said, do double-check for spider-mite infestation (see page 225) as the symptoms can be similar.

Dahlia mosaic virus causes yellowing along the veins or in the centre of the leaf, and the accurately named spotted wilt virus causes wilting in addition to mottling. If your plants have a virus, pull them up and burn them rather than putting them on the compost heap. There is no cure and, if left, they risk infecting the rest of your stock.

## GALL

This is a disease where the crown of the tuber starts to proliferate into cauliflower-like masses of knobbly distorted growth. Gall is caused by bacteria entering the plant through a wound and triggering the cells to multiply rapidly in an uncontrolled fashion. There is nothing to do but throw the plant away, together with the compost it was growing in.

# GLOSSARY

**AGM** The Award of Garden Merit, presented by the Royal Horticultural Society, indicates that the plant is recommended by the Society and will perform well in the garden.

**Anther** The pollen sac at the end of the stamen.

**Apical, Apical bud** The main flower at the top of the stem, from 'apex' meaning the highest part of something. The term is also used for the apical shoot, meaning the top or leading shoot.

**Bicolour** Having two colours.

**Capitulum** A dense cluster of small flowers, a compact flowerhead.

**Cultivar** A cultivated form of the plant selected for its desirable characteristics.

**Deadheading** Removing spent flowers from the plant to encourage more blooms.

**Dinner-Plate** A term for the very largest dahlia sizes.

**Disbud** The practice of removing flower buds while they are still unopened, to influence those that remain.

**Disc florets** Small tubular flowers that make up the central disc in dahlias and other plants in the family Asteraceae.

**Dwarf** A smaller-than-usual cultivar of a plant. In dahlias, this is understood as being 60cm (24in) or less in height.

**Eyes** The buds on a tuber from which the next year's growth will originate.

**Fimbriated** The term used for the feathered or fringed effect at the end of the petals in some dahlia cultivars.

**Hybrid** A genetic cross between two different species, genera or cultivars.

**Inflorescence** The complete flowerhead, including stems, petals, bracts, reproductive organs and all other elements.

**Laciniated** See Fimbriated.

**Language of flowers** Otherwise known as floriography, this was popular with the Victorians, who attributed flowers with meanings so that they could send cryptic messages to one another.

**Lateral bud** A bud located on the side of the stem, usually in the leaf axil where the leaf joins the stem. These are usually smaller than the apical bud.

**Open pollination** Uncontrolled pollination between similar plants in the garden or field, where the offspring may differ from the parent due to the introduction of new genes.

**Plasticity** The tendency of individuals of the same genetic make-up to look different from each other when grown under different conditions.

**Potash** The horticultural term for the element Potassium (K) in water-soluble form. The name comes from the original practice of collecting wood ashes in a container.

**Ray floret** Also known as a ligulate floret, this is a small, strap-shaped flower that, together with a number of others, forms the ray around the central disc in the composite flowers of the Asteraceae.

**Receptacle** The thickened part at the top of a stem to which the floral organs are attached.

**Species** A population of individuals that have a high level of genetic similarity and which can interbreed.

**Sport** A spontaneously arising mutation in part of a plant that can then be reproduced vegetatively as a new cultivar.

**Stamen** The pollen-producing (male) reproductive organ of a flower. It consists of a filament and anther.

**Tricolour** Having three colours.

**Tuber** A thickened underground stem that serves as a food-storage organ and bears buds from which new growth arises.

**Variety** A classification of cultivated plants, below sub-species, where there are minor but distinctive and inheritable characteristics exhibited.

**Vegetative propagation** The process by which plants produce genetically identical new individuals, or clones.

# INDEX

# NAOMI'S ACKNOWLEDGEMENTS

## This book is dedicated to Holly, who loves dahlias.

I would like to thank my husband, Chris Wlaznik, whose endless support and encouragement allows me to climb ever higher mountains, and my children for their enduring tolerance of my obsession with writing and plants.

Mike Mann, Louise Danks and Mark Twyning at the National Collection of Dahlias in Cornwall have been fantastic, as has Jon Wheatley. Thank you for your guidance, read-throughs and quick turnaround answers – I hope you all like the book!

My proofreaders have been magnificent in their perspective, eagle eyes and constructive criticism: Morwenna Slade and Chris Wlaznik, as always; Andrew O'Brien who proved himself a dark horse in this department, and Philippa Burrough who deserves a mention both for her kind proofreading and thoughts on planting combinations. It would have been a lesser book without you all. Thanks, too, to Carol Wlaznik for lending me large chunks of her garden for horticultural experimentation and to all those fantastic and talented friends, florists and gardeners who have let me pick their brains, observe their professional handiwork and been thoroughly supportive over the years.

The team at Pavilion has been fantastic: Krissy Mallett, Bella Cockrell, Katie Cowan and Polly Powell have worked tirelessly and making this beautiful book has been a pleasure alongside the rest of the team – Diana Vowles, Hilary Mandleberg with her marvellous editorial input, the illustrative talents of Somang Lee and the deft design work of Michelle Mac and Gail Jones.

Finally, special mention must go to Georgianna Lane for her tireless pursuit of the most sumptuous dahlias and her thoroughly gorgeous pictures. I have loved working in partnership on this and look forward to our next project!

# GEORGIANNA'S ACKNOWLEDGEMENTS

The stunning dahlias that appear here were photographed in England and the USA at a variety of field locations and, as cut flowers, in my own studios.

The breadth of variety in the resulting images would not have been possible without the generous and enthusiastic contributions of experts Mike Mann, Mark Twyning and Louise Danks at the National Dahlia Collection in Cornwall. They truly saved the day by granting me full access to photograph the expansive collection, answering myriad questions and guiding the selection of varieties to be featured.

In the USA, field shots came from Swan Island Dahlias in Oregon and from the beautiful private garden of Alicia Schwede of Flirty Fleurs.

Many thanks to everyone at the Seattle Wholesale Growers Market, especially Diane Szukovathy and Dennis Westphall of Jello Mold Farm, and Molly and Danielle, who helped me source and purchase buckets of gorgeous, sustainably grown blooms.

My partner in this flowery adventure, author Naomi Slade, has been an absolute joy to work with. I'm certain that readers will be captivated by her witty and informative text, and by the trove of delightful anecdotes and historical details she uncovered about the individual varieties.

David Phillips, my husband and fellow photographer, has provided unfailingly positive support and often desperately needed hands-on assistance in the field, including heroically locating specific blooms undamaged by the savage weather we experienced in Cornwall.

Thank you, as ever, to my family for being endlessly patient with my erratic schedule, frequent spur-of-the-moment travel and general state of distraction when working on deadline.

And my deep appreciation to Publisher Polly Powell, Publishing Director Katie Cowan, Commissioning Editor Krissy Mallett, Editor Bella Cockrell, and Designers Michelle Mac and Gail Jones of Pavilion Books for envisioning this exceptional book and entrusting me to photograph it.